W9-DEA-487

EveryDay Quotations

EveryDay Quotations

Just the Right Words for
Life's Memorable Occasions

Edited by Jack Maguire

A ROUNDTABLE PRESS BOOK

Doubleday Direct, Inc.
Garden City, New York

A season is set for everything, a time for every experience under heaven.
A time for being born and a time for dying,
A time for planting and a time for uprooting the planted;
A time for slaying and a time for healing,
A time for tearing down and a time for building up;
A time for weeping and a time for laughing,
A time for wailing and a time for dancing;
A time for throwing stones and a time for gathering stones;
A time for embracing and a time for shunning embraces;
A time for seeking and a time for losing,
A time for keeping and a time for discarding;
A time for ripping and a time for sewing,
A time for silence and a time for speaking;
A time for loving and a time for hating;
A time for war and a time for peace.

—BIBLE, ECCLESIASTES 3:1–8

Contents

Acknowledgments

To ensure a wide-ranging, intriguing, and distinctive selection of quotations, the lines, poems, and passages that appear in *EveryDay Quotations* were chosen from more than a hundred different sources. Most of these sources were books, although especially relevant or interesting quotations were taken from reputable periodicals and television and radio programs as well.

Any large collection of quotations inevitably draws on previously published collections, if only to help guarantee accuracy and an appropriate variety of quotes pertaining to each subject. Among the general quotation books that proved especially valuable in the creation of *EveryDay Quotations* were the following:

Andrews, Robert, ed. *The Columbia Dictionary of Quotations.* New York: Columbia University Press, 1993.

Auden, W.H., and Louis Kronenberger. *The Viking Book of Aphorisms.* New York: Viking, 1962.

Braude, Jacob M. *Speaker's Encyclopedia.* Englewood Cliffs, N.J.: Prentice-Hall, Inc., 1955.

Byrne, Robert. *The Fourth 637 Best Things Anybody Ever Said*. New York: Fawcett Crest, 1990.

———. *The Other 637 Best Things Anybody Ever Said*. New York: Fawcett Crest, 1984.

———. *The 637 Best Things Anybody Ever Said*. New York: Fawcett Crest, 1982.

Cohen, J.M., and M.J. Cohen, eds. *The Penguin Dictionary of Quotations*. New York: Penguin, 1960.

Cole, William, ed. *Poems for Seasons and Celebrations*. New York: World Publishing Co., 1961.

Cordello, Becky Stevens. *Celebrations*. New York: Butterick Publishing, 1977.

Gross, John, ed. *The Oxford Book of Aphorisms*. New York: Oxford University Press, 1983.

Krythe, Maymie R. *All About American Holidays*. New York: Harper & Brothers, 1962.

Prochnow, Herbert V., and Herbert V. Prochnow, Jr. *The Public Speaker's Treasure Chest*. New York: Harper & Row, 1977.

Roberts, Elizabeth, and Elias Amidon, eds. *Earth Prayers*. HarperSanFrancisco, 1991.

Roberts, Kate Louise, ed. *Hoyt's New Cyclopedia of Practical Quotations*. New York and London: Funk and Wagnalls, 1922.

Rowes, Barbara. *The Book of Quotes*. New York: E.P. Dutton, 1979.

Safransky, Sy, ed. *Sunbeams*. Berkeley, Calif.: North Atlantic Books, 1990.

Sampson, Anthony, and Sally Sampson, eds. *The Oxford Book of Ages*. New York: Oxford University Press, 1985.

Schauffler, Robert Haven, ed. *The Days We Celebrate*. Vol. 1, *Celebrations for Christmas and Other High Days*. Vol. 2, *Celebrations for Festivals*. Vol. 3, *Celebrations for Patriotic Days*. Vol. 4, *Celebrations for Special Occasions*. New York: Dodd, Mead & Co., 1954, 1954, 1955, 1956.

Spiegelman, Art, and Bob Schneider, eds. *Whole Grains.* New York: Douglas Links, 1973.

Stevenson, Burton. *The Home Book of Quotations: Classical and Modern.* New York: Dodd, Mead and Company, 1934.

Tripp, Rhoda Thomas. *The International Thesaurus of Quotations.* New York: Thomas Y. Crowell Co., 1970.

Uris, Dorothy. *Say It Again.* New York: E.P. Dutton, 1979.

Walsh, William S. *International Encyclopedia of Prose and Poetical Quotations.* New York: Greenwood Press, 1968.

Winokur, Jon. *True Confessions.* New York: Penguin, 1993.

Among the Christian-oriented quotation collections that served as good resources for this book were the following:

Braybrooke, Neville. *A Partridge in a Pear Tree.* Westminster, Md.: The Newman Press, 1960.

Goudge, Elizabeth. *A Book of Comfort.* New York: Coward-McCann, Inc., 1964.

———. *A Book of Faith.* New York: Coward, McCann, and Geoghegan, Inc., 1976.

Kauffman, Donald T., ed. *A Treasury of Great Prayers.* Westwood, N.J.: Fleming H. Revell Company, 1964.

Llewellyn, Miller, ed. *The Joy of Christmas.* New York: Bobbs-Merrill, 1960.

Works on Jewish themes that provided valuable assistance included:

Baron, Joseph L., ed. *A Treasury of Jewish Quotations.* New York: Crown Publishers, Inc., 1956.

Gibetz, Jessica. *Wise Words.* New York: William Morrow and Company, Inc., 1997.

Hertzberg, Arthur, ed. *Judaism.* New York: George Braziller, 1962.

Strassfield, Michael. *The Jewish Holidays*. New York: Harper & Row, 1985.

Trepp, Leo. *The Complete Book of Jewish Observance*. New York: Simon & Schuster, 1980.

Good sources for quotations pertaining to women's experience included:

Ostle, M.G. *The Note Books of a Woman Alone*. London: J. M. Dent and Sons, Ltd., 1935.

Washbourn, Penelope. *Seasons of Woman*. San Francisco: Harper & Row, 1979.

Sources often consulted for quotations relating to African-American experience included:

Cowan, Tom, and Jack Maguire. *Timelines of African-American History*. New York: Berkley, 1994.

Riley, Dorothy W., ed. *My Soul Looks Back, Lest I Forget*. New York: Harper Collins, 1993.

Other specialized collections that proved useful for different parts of this book were the following:

Brewton, Sara, and John E. Brewton. *Birthday Candles Burning Bright*. New York: Macmillan & Company, 1960.

Handley, Helen, and Andra Samuelson, eds. *Child*. New York: W.W. Norton Co., 1992.

Ickis, Marguerite. *The Book of Patriotic Holidays*. New York: Dodd, Mead & Company, 1962.

Lansbury, Angela. *Wedding Speeches and Toasts*. London: Warl Lock Ltd., 1988.

Lewis, Linda Rannells. *Birthdays*. Boston: Little, Brown, 1976.

O'Farrell, Padraic. *Irish Toasts, Curses, & Blessings.* New York: Sterling Publishing Co., Inc., 1995.
Stotter, Ruth, ed. *One Hundred Memorable Quotes About Stories and Storytelling.* Stinson Beach, Calif.: Stotter Press, 1995.

I am especially grateful to Marsha Melnick of Roundtable Press for helping to shape this project and for bringing her considerable talents and wisdom to the quote selection process. I am also thankful for the expert assistance of Tom Cowan in collecting many of the entries.

Introduction

A quotation at the right moment is like
bread in a famine.

—Talmud

The desire to celebrate fulfills a basic human need. Whether we're getting together for an anniversary party or a Thanksgiving dinner, an Easter brunch or a housewarming, a victory bash or a retirement banquet, we feel compelled to express ourselves more powerfully, not only to give the event itself greater style and structure but also to guarantee that it lives on more vitally in our memories. At such times, we want to be sure to say the right thing, whether it's wise, witty, compassionate, insightful, or just plain funny.

Fortunately, many of the right things have already been said, and you can take advantage of this fact. It is a time-honored practice to pass along quotations that have already proven their value. Even great wordsmiths, from William Shakespeare to Mae West, frequently recycled statements that were popular sayings in their day. *EveryDay Quotations* is a uniquely varied collection of more than six hundred time-tested quotations that you can use to enrich the days, weeks, months, and seasons of your life.

EveryDay Quotations empowers you to bring a special touch

of humor, grace, drama, or heart to virtually any cause for celebration. The entries are conveniently organized according to days, themes, or types of occasions, with plenty of cross-referencing to give you the maximum number of possible quotes to consider using. Here you'll find quotations for personal rites of passage, such as birthdays, coming-of-age ceremonies, graduations, weddings, reunions, and memorial services, as well as for religious and cultural holidays, such as Christmas, Passover, St. Patrick's Day, Valentine's Day, Father's Day, Fourth of July, and so on. The author of the quote is cited below it, and in certain cases, the work in which the quote appears is also cited.

The quotations provided for each occasion vary in mood, length, statement, tone, and style so that you can select the most appropriate ones to use for your specific purposes. Some entries are pithy one-liners; others are more extensive commentaries. Some are from the famous; others from the infamous. Some are classic; others contemporary. The multicultural mix includes poems, scriptural excerpts, anecdotes, philosophical musings, fables, humorous remarks, healing blessings, and inspirational words of wisdom that either address the occasion straightforwardly or allude to it in a more general manner, by pursuing broader themes that can easily be associated with it.

Above all, *EveryDay Quotations* is a book made for delightful browsing. In addition to providing memorable words that you can share directly with others, it gives you fascinating ideas and insights to ponder all on your own.

Maybe you won't actually incorporate a particular quotation into your dinner party talk, or a speech you're making, or a toast you're giving, or a letter you're writing. Nevertheless, it can still capture your imagination, enabling you to see the occasion in a new light, and to enjoy it in a fresh way.

Perhaps the quotation will inspire you to find your own original way of expressing yourself. For example, a memory piece you read in these pages about someone else's mother may move you to develop a reminiscence of your own mother that you can pass along to her and the rest of your family on Mother's Day, or on her birthday, or on any occasion when she's being honored or recalled.

When you do want to share a quotation from this book on a special occasion, bear in mind these guidelines:

When speaking, it's usually more effective to quote from memory than to read from the book. In advance of the occasion, learn the quote you've chosen by repeating it to yourself every so often. However, if you prefer to use the text for a longer piece, or if you're not reasonably confident about how well you'll remember the quote when the time comes, by all means do read from the book. It's better to get the quote right by reading it than to bungle it all on your own.

When writing a quotation in a card, it's usually more effective to let the quotation stand alone and speak for itself. Think of the quotation as a little gift that you are passing along with the card—a gift that the receiver is free to enjoy as he or she wishes. If you're incorporating the quote into a longer personal note or letter, you may still want to let the quotation stand alone. In this context, however, you have more scope to connect the quote to your own sentiments in a manner that your reader may find very gratifying.

For any one occasion when you'll be talking, it's a good idea to select two or three items to quote. If you're delivering a speech, two or three quotations can provide refreshing breaks from your own language. If you simply want to prepare yourself ahead of time to be a more entertaining conversationalist, then two or three quotes can provide you with more options to suit the way the conversation is flowing.

In any event, different quotes appeal to different listeners.

When you have two or three quotes to share instead of one, you increase your chances of giving everyone something to remember.

In choosing a quote for a particular occasion, consider in advance the people who will be there and the most likely mood or tone of the gathering. Ask yourself such questions: What is the age range of the people who will be there? What are their educational backgrounds? What are their interests in life? What kinds of humor might appeal to all of them? How are they most likely to be feeling? How will they most likely behave? You may not know *all* the answers, but *any* conclusions you can draw will help you make an appropriate quotation choice.

Determine ahead of time exactly when you might share the quote. If the quotation belongs in a speech you're giving at a preset time, you already know when you'll deliver it. However, if you're just hoping to be able to pass along the quotation sometime during the occasion, it helps to plan in advance—as much as you can—the best possible times for doing so. In most cases, these will be times when everyone is fairly settled, gathered close together, and not too preoccupied with other matters, such as greeting each other, gathering food, or viewing photographs. The more you can anticipate good opportunities, the better the odds are that you'll actually have one and use it.

Most often when speaking, it's best to begin with a quote rather than to back into it. Quotations are excellent attention getters. To preface them with too many remarks robs them of their "striking" power. For this reason, it's usually best to state them directly, *then* (if necessary) to explain or expand. In the context of a longer speech, you can afford to be more flexible about this general rule, timing quotations according to the way they best relate to your main points and the overall rhythm of your delivery.

Don't alter the quotation to suit your purposes. The quote you are using has already earned its memorability. You don't want to tamper with this quality—and, perhaps, set in motion a mistaken version of the quotation—by changing it to suit your particular taste or interests. Instead, you need to respect the original speaker by quoting his or her words *exactly*.

You can always follow up the quotation with remarks of your own that connect it more explicitly with the occasion at hand, or that correct certain word usages that you find obscure or irritating. For example, if you're bothered by the fact that a quotation refers to human beings in general as "men," you can say something like this afterward: "Of course, I'd like this quote even more if it said 'people' instead of just 'men,' but we know it means that!"

The previous example of an awkward gender-reference problem relates to a bigger issue involving quotations in general and, therefore, the representative sampling of quotations that appears in this collection. Because of male dominance throughout most of human history, far more attention has been paid to the words of men than the words of women. As a result, most quotations offered in virtually all comprehensive quotation source books are attributed to men.

To help rectify this imbalance, special care has been taken in *EveryDay Quotations* to include a high percentage of entries attributed to women in each of the quote categories. Similar efforts have been made to represent a wide variety of ethnic and social backgrounds.

Holidays and major life events are precisely the times when we most want to overcome the barriers that separate us and to find common cause for celebration. Today the pace of life is more hectic than it's ever been, and we're forced to spend more time away from our family members, friends, and neighbors than people did in the past. We count upon ceremonial rituals to make time stand still for a moment and to bring human beings back together. *EveryDay Quotations* provides essential material for creating this kind of extraordinary experience and communion. May you derive much pleasure from it, and pass that pleasure along to your listeners!

Quotations

Aging

(also see BIRTHDAY, COMING OF AGE)

Many times it's not the actual age we've reached that impresses us, or that gives us a sense of identity, or that's truly worth celebrating. Instead, it's the process of aging we've gone through—the journey we've made from one physical, emotional, spiritual, and/or occupational era in our lives to another.

This same process also fascinates and instructs us when we consider the lives of people we've known for a long time. No matter what they may be like right now, or how they might appear to someone just meeting them, their images in our minds and hearts include touches of who they were when we first encountered them, and what they were like at various important life stages between then and now.

This category, Aging, offers statements about the aging process that go beyond reference to a single birthday or, in many cases, even a single era in life. The entries proceed chronologically: first quotes referring mainly to childhood, then quotes referring mainly to youth and middle age, and finally quotes referring mainly to old age. The last group, old age, includes the most quotes—an acknowledgment of the unique wisdom that comes after an entire lifetime, and of the many occasions when we're moved to honor the continuing presence in our lives of elder friends, family members, and associates.

An Aging quote can be appropriate for any occasion that somehow involves celebrating a particular period of life. A quote that focuses on *childhood,* for example, could be spoken at a gathering for a child's birthday, or for Mother's or Father's Day, depending on how well it fits the circumstances.

A quote addressing *youth* could be delivered at a young person's birthday, coming-of-age or naming ceremony, confirmation, or commencement. The young person may even want to deliver it as a personal statement, depending on his or her level of maturity.

A quote regarding *middle age* could be shared at an individual's fortieth through sixty-fourth birthday party (using the U.S. Census Bureau's definition of middle age), or at any other time when he or she is being roasted, paid tribute to, or reunited with peers. A particular quote may be especially appropriate for the middle-aged honoree him- or herself to communicate, as a means of joining in the festivities.

A quote involving *old age* could be given at a birthday gathering, retirement celebration, or recognition party for someone more than 65 years old, or at an event that brings together a group of people in that age range. Elders who are so often called upon to communicate what they've learned in life can also benefit from having a quote in mind that reflects how they think or feel.

———

And even if you were in some prison, the walls of which let none of the sounds of the world come to your senses—would you not then still have your childhood, that precious, kingly possession, that treasure-house of memories?

—*Rainer Maria Rilke*

It is quite easy for me to think of a God of love mainly because I grew up in a family where love was central and where lovely relationships were ever present. It is quite easy for me to think of the universe as basically friendly, mainly because of my uplifting hereditary and environmental circumstances. It is quite easy for me to lean more toward optimism than pessimism about human nature, mainly because of my childhood experiences.

—*Martin Luther King, Jr.*
(speech given at Crozer
Theological Seminary,
Chester, PA, 1949)

The end of childhood is when things cease to astonish us. When the world seems familiar, when one has got used to existence, one has become an adult.

—*Eugene Ionesco*

Every child's sense of himself is terrifyingly fragile. He is at the mercy of his elders, and when he finds himself totally at the mercy of his peers, who know as little about themselves as he, it is because his elders have abandoned him. I am talking, then, about morale, that sense of self with which the child must be invested. No child can do it alone. Children, I submit, cannot be fooled. They can only be betrayed by adults.

—*James Baldwin*
(Dark Days)

The childhood shows the man
As morning shows the day.

—*John Milton*
(Paradise Regained)

Gather ye Rose-buds while ye may,
Old Time is still a-flying:
And this same flower that smiles to day,
Tomorrow will be dying.

—*Robert Herrick*

Live as long as you may, the first twenty years are the longest half of your life.

—*Robert Southey*
(The Doctor)

You're only young once, and if you work it right, once is enough.

—*Joe E. Lewis*

We are not unlike a particularly hardy crustacean. . . . With each passage from one stage of human growth to the next, we, too, must shed a protective structure. We are left exposed and vulnerable—but also yeasty and embryonic again, capable of stretching in ways we hadn't known before. These sheddings may take several years or more. Coming out of each passage, though, we enter a longer and more stable period in which we can expect relative tranquility and a sense of equilibrium regained.

—*Gail Sheehy* (Passages)

Life is all memory, except for the one present moment that goes by so quick you hardly catch it going.

—*Tennessee Williams*

Live decently, fearlessly, joyously—and don't forget that in the long run, it is not the years in your life but the life in your years that counts.

—*Adlai Stevenson*

Because aging is a "crisis of the imagination," our attitudes can transform the experience.

—*Jane O'Reilly*

Middle age is when your age starts to show around your middle.

—*Bob Hope*

The really frightening thing about middle age is the knowledge that you'll outgrow it.

—*Doris Day*

No wise man ever wished to be younger.

—*Jonathan Swift*

Middle age is when you've met so many people that every new person you meet reminds you of someone else.

—*Ogden Nash*

That fatal ten years between thirty-five and forty-five is neither youth nor age; the beauty of youth is declined and the beauty of age is not yet arrived.

—*Katherine Anne Porter*
(letter, 1959)

The first forty years of life furnish the text, while the remaining thirty supply the commentary.

—*Arthur Schopenhauer*
(Counsels and Maxims)

From thirty to forty-five runs the stage in which a man normally finds all his ideas, the first principles, at least, of that ideology which he is to make his own. After forty-five he devotes himself to the full development of the inspirations he has had between thirty and forty-five.

—*Jose Ortega y Gasset*

Everyone has talent at twenty-five, the difficulty is to have it at fifty.

—*Edgar Degas*

At past fifty, Adams solemnly and painfully learned to ride the bicycle.

—*Henry Adams*
(The Education of
Henry Adams)

The years between fifty and seventy are the hardest. You are always being asked to do things, and yet you are not decrepit enough to turn them down.

—*T.S. Eliot*

Everybody wants to live longer but nobody wants to grow old.

—*Jules Rostand*

Most people say that as you get old, you have to give up things. . . . I think you get old because you give up things.
—*Theodore Francis Green*

I guess the best assurance of a long life is to get yourself a set of long-living parents like I did.
—*Harry Truman*

Old age comes at a bad time.
—*Sue Banducci*

You're never too old to become younger.
—*Mae West*

Old age is like climbing a mountain. You climb from ledge to ledge. The higher you get, the more tired and breathless you become, but your view becomes much more extensive.
—*Ingmar Bergman*

You are as young as your faith, as old as your doubt; as young as your self-confidence, as old as your fear; as young as your hope, as old as your despair.
—*Samuel Ullman*

Who would have guessed that maturity is only a short break in adolescence?
—*Jules Feiffer*

Youth is not chronological age but the state of growing, learning, changing. . . . All people must be helped to regain the condition of youth.

—*Charles Reich*

To be old is a glorious thing when one has not unlearned what it means to begin.

—*Martin Buber*

I was a hard student until I entered on the business of life, the duties of which leave no idle time to those disposed to fulfill them; and now, retired, and at the age of seventy-six, I am again a hard student.

—*Thomas Jefferson*
(letter, 1819)

The seas are quiet when the winds give o'er
So calm are we when passions are no more.
For then we know how vain it was to boast
Of fleeting things, so certain to be lost.
Clouds of affection from our younger eyes
Conceal that emptiness which age descries.

The soul's dark cottage, batter'd and decay'd
Lets in new light through chinks that Time hath made:
Stronger by weakness, wiser men become
As they draw near to their eternal home
Leaving the old, both worlds at once they view
That stand upon the threshold of the new.

—*Edmund Waller*

Youth is a quality, not a matter of circumstances.
—*Frank Lloyd Wright*

If the very old will remember, the very young will listen.
—*Chief Dan George*

The three ages of man: youth, middle age, and "You're looking wonderful!"
—*Francis Cardinal Spellman*

Men of age object too much, consult too long, adventure too little, repent too soon.
—*Francis Bacon*

He is the happiest man who can trace an unbroken connection between the end of his life and the beginning.
—*Johann Wolfgang von Goethe* (Maxims and Reflections)

Can I still make myself useful? That one may legitimately ask, and I think that I can answer "yes." I feel that I may be useful in a more personal, more direct way than ever before. I have, though how I do not know, acquired much wisdom. . . . It is quite wrong to think of old age as a downward slope. One climbs higher and higher with the advancing years, that too, with surprising strides.
—*George Sand*

Nothing is more incumbent on the old, than to know when they shall get out of the way, and relinquish to younger successors the honours they can no longer earn, and the duties they can no longer perform.

—Thomas Jefferson
(letter, 1815)

Anniversary

(also see VALENTINE'S DAY, WEDDING)

Most often, a wedding anniversary is an intimate affair. Couples celebrate it alone, or with their immediate family members, or with a few, very close friends. On the other hand, a tenth, twenty-fifth, or fiftieth wedding anniversary—or, for that matter, any anniversary year divisible by 5—can prompt a huge circus of a party, with as many guests as the partygiver's resources allow.

The quotes below were chosen with these contrasting scenarios in mind. Some of the quotes—because of their realistic honesty or intimate emotion—may strike you as most appropriate to share on a one-to-one basis with your own spouse, or to pass along to the celebrating couple in a small gathering involving very close loved ones. Other quotes may seem far more appropriate for a large gathering that invites broad humor and age-old verities.

In collecting entries for the "Anniversary" category, greater preference was given to quotes that speak philosophically of marriage as an adventure or accomplishment than to quotes that simply express love between two people. For more of the latter kind of quote, check out the Valentine's Day and Wedding categories.

Effective ways to deliver a quote at an anniversary gathering are as part of a toast, as a preface (or aftermath) to gift-giving, or in the context of general remarks after eating. If you are sharing the quote with your spouse, you may want to surprise him or her with it early in the day, when you first offer your "happy anniversary" wishes, or else at the close of the day, when both of you are likely to be feeling quite mellow about each other. An anniversary quote also makes a nice addition to an anniversary card, party invitation, or written tribute.

The art of love . . . is largely the art of persistence.
— *Dr. Albert Ellis*

Love at first sight is easy to understand. It's when two people have been looking at each other for years that it becomes a miracle.
— *Sam Levenson*

One resents any change, even though one knows that transformation is natural and part of the process of life and its evolution. Like its parallel in physical passion, the early ecstatic stage of a relationship cannot continue always at the same pitch of intensity. It moves to another phase of growth which one should not dread, but welcome as one welcomes summer after spring.

— *Anne Morrow Lindbergh*
(Gift from the Sea)

Loyalty is the holiest good in the human heart.
> —*Seneca* (Epistulae ad
> Lucilium, *Epis. 88, 29)*

Once the realization is accepted that even between the closest human beings infinite distances continue to exist, a wonderful living side by side can grow up, if they succeed in loving the distance between them which makes it possible for each to see the other whole against the sky.
> —*Rainer Maria Rilke*

Chains do not hold a marriage together. It is threads, hundreds of tiny threads which sew people together through the years. That is what makes a marriage last—more than passion or even sex!
> —*Simone Signoret*

Wasn't marriage, like life, unstimulating and unprofitable and somewhat empty when too well ordered and protected and guarded? Wasn't it finer, more splendid, more nourishing, when it was, like life itself, a mixture of the sordid and the magnificent; of mud and stars; of earth and flowers; of love and hate and laughter and tears and ugliness and beauty and hurt?
> —*Edna Ferber*

Success in marriage does not come merely through finding the right mate, but through being the right mate.
> —*Barnett R. Brickner*

Trusty, dusky, vivid true,
With eyes of good and bramble-dew,
Steel true and blade-straight,
The greater artificer
Made my mate.

Honour, anger, valour, fire;
A love that life could never tire,
Death quench or evil stir,
The mighty master
Gave to her.

Teacher, tender, comrade, wife,
A fellow-farer true through life,
Heart-whole and soul-free,
The august father
Gave to me.

—*Robert Louis Stevenson*

A successful marriage is not a gift, it is an achievement.
—*Ann Landers*

That married couples can live together day after day is a miracle the Vatican has overlooked.
—*Bill Cosby*

Here's to marriage, that happy estate that resembles a pair of scissors: so joined that they cannot be separated, often moving in opposite directions, yet punishing anyone who comes between them.
—*Sydney Smith*

Let me not to the marriage of true minds
Admit impediments. Love is not love
Which alters when it alteration finds
Or bends with the remover to remove;
O, no! it is an ever-fixed mark,
That looks on tempests and is never shaken;
It is the star to every wand'ring bark,
Whose worth's unknown, although his height be taken.
Love's not Time's fool, though rosy lips and cheeks
Within his bending sickle's compass come;
Love alters not with his brief hours and weeks,
But bears it out even to the edge of doom.
    If this be error and upon me proved,
    I never writ, nor no man ever loved.

—*William Shakespeare*
(Sonnet 116)

Immature love says: "I love you because I need you." Mature love says: "I need you because I love you."

—*Erich Fromm*

Love is what you've been through with somebody.

—*James Thurber*

Marriage is three parts love and seven parts forgiveness of sins.

—*Langdon Mitchell*

Autumn

(also see THANKSGIVING DAY)

Going by the sun, moon, and stars, autumn begins around September 22 (the autumn equinox), and lasts until around December 21 (the winter solstice). Going by most people's schedules, however, autumn begins after Labor Day (the first Monday in September) and lasts until after Thanksgiving (the fourth Thursday in November). That amounts to almost four months during which autumn quotes remain appropriate!

Here are words to share at autumn campfires, harvest festivals, county fair picnics, back-to-school gatherings, and, of course, Thanksgiving get-togethers.

For man, autumn is a time of harvest, of getting together.
For nature, it is a time of sowing, of scattering abroad.
                                                    —*Edwin Way Teale*

Season of mists and mellow fruitfulness,
Close bosom-friend of the maturing sun;
Conspiring with him how to load and bless
With fruit the vines that round the thatch-eaves run;
To bend with apples the moss'd cottage-trees,
And fill all fruit with ripeness to the core.
　　　　　　　—*John Keats*
　　　　　　　　("To Autumn")

It was Autumn, and incessant
　Piped the quails from shocks and sheaves,
And, like living coals, the apples
　Burned among the withering leaves.
　　　　　　　—*Henry Wadsworth*
　　　　　　　　Longfellow

O Autumn, laden with fruit, and stained
With the blood of the grape, pass not, but sit
Beneath my shady roof; there thou may'st rest
And tune thy jolly voice to my fresh pipe,
And all the daughters of the year shall dance!
Sing now the lusty song of fruit and flowers.
　　　　　　　—*William Blake*
　　　　　　　　("To Autumn")

O, it sets my heart a clickin' like the tickin' of a clock
When the frost is on the punkin and the fodder's in the
　shock.
　　　　　　　—*James Whitcomb Riley*

Baby Shower/ New Baby

These quotes provide a number of different points of view on that miracle of miracles, the birth of a child. As befits the subject, some of these are warm and cuddly, others frank and provocative.

The former kind of quotes can be shared on virtually any occasion involving a new baby, from a baby shower to a birth celebration to a cradle party. The latter kind may also be appropriate for these occasions, depending on the personality of the mother or mother-to-be and the other people present. If not, they can be passed along from friend or family member to new mother or mother-to-be at more intimate times.

"Monday's Child" is included here because it's a classic poem relating to childbirth. It offers a delightful sentiment for acknowledging a birth that occurred on a Monday, Tuesday, Friday, Saturday (possibly), or Sunday. Otherwise, you may want to choose another quote!

Children are still the way you were as a child, sad like that and happy—and if you think of your childhood, you live among them again.

—*Rainer Maria Rilke*

Birth is not one act. It is a process.

—*Erich Fromm*

Monday's child is fair of face,
Tuesday's child is full of grace,
Wednesday's child is full of woe,
Thursday's child has far to go,
Friday's child is loving and giving,
Saturday's child works hard for a living,
And the child that is born on the Sabbath day
Is bonny and blithe, and good and gay.

—*Anonymous*

Every child begins the world again. . . .

—*Henry David Thoreau*

Where did you come from, baby dear?
Out of the everywhere into here.
Where did you get your eyes so blue?
Out of the sky as I came through.

—*George Macdonald*

I was happy to have children. I had always intended to have children. Not only because having "my own"—and "our own":

because I knew that my husband, whoever he was to be, would want and care for and richly love them too—would stand up at such a joyous thing, but also because I respected and marveled at and admired my body. I wanted my body to do something its composition suggested it was supposed to do. I did not want my body to fail. I wanted my body, as well as my mind and spirit, to succeed, to reach an appropriate glory.

—*Gwendolyn Brooks*
(Report from Part One)

Children make you want to start life over.
—*Muhammad Ali*
(The Greatest)

Nowadays babies get up and walk soon's you drop 'em, but twenty years ago when I was a girl babies stayed babies longer.
—*Toni Morrison*
(*a character in* Beloved)

When you came into the world, my last born, Minet-Cherie, I suffered for three days and two nights. When I was carrying you I was as big as a house. Three days seems a long time. The beasts put us to shame, we women who can no longer bear our children joyfully. But I've never regretted my suffering. They do say that children like you, who have been carried so high in the womb and have taken so long to come down into the daylight, are always the children that are most loved, because they have lain so near their mother's heart and have been so unwilling to leave her.

—*Colette* (My Mother's House
and Sido)

Childbirth is more admirable than conquest, more amazing than self-defense, and as courageous as either one.
—*Gloria Steinem*

The character of a child is already plain, even in its mother's womb. Before I was born my mother was in great agony of spirit and in a tragic situation. She could take no food except iced oysters and champagne. If people ask me when I began to dance I reply, "In my mother's womb, probably as a result of the oysters and champagne—the food of Aphrodite."
—*Isadora Duncan*
(My Life)

Beginning

So many occasions in life involve the challenge and excitement of *beginning* something. Among them are the start of a new athletic season, cultural season, school year, business year, or way of life; the launching of a boat, project, campaign, or company; an engagement, marriage, contract signing, or merger; a housewarming, groundbreaking, dedication, or consecration; a confirmation, coming-of-age, commencement, or investiture.

Here are a wide variety of quotes to use on any of these occasions. Choose among them according to the particular "beginning" attributes you wish to emphasize: freshness, courage, humility, daring, persistence, hope, patience . . . or the eventual ending.

We learn by going where we have to go.
—*Theodore Roethke*

The grace to be a beginner is always the best prayer for an artist. The beginner's humility and openness lead to exploration. Exploration leads to accomplishment. All of it begins at the beginning, with the first small and scary step.

—*Julia Cameron*
(The Artist's Way)

At a certain point, you have to go to the edge of the cliff and jump—put your ideas into a form, share that form with others.

—*Meredith Monk*

Life shrinks or expands in proportion to one's courage.

—*Anaïs Nin*

And the trouble is if you don't risk anything, you risk even more.

—*Erica Jong*

He that will not sail till all dangers are over must never put to sea.

—*Thomas Fuller*

To persevere, trusting in what hopes he has
is courage in a man. The coward despairs.

—*Euripides*

Lift up your hearts. Each new hour holds new chances for new beginnings.

—*Maya Angelou*

We can't do great things. We can only do small things with great love.

—*Mother Teresa*

Nothing will ever be attempted, if all possible objections must be first overcome.

—*Dr. Samuel Johnson*
(Rasselas)

There is an old saying "well begun is half done"—'tis a bad one. I would use instead—Not begun at all until half done.

—*John Keats (letter, 1817)*

Never undertake anything unless you have the heart to ask Heaven's blessing on your undertaking!

—*Georg Christoph*
Lichtenberg (Aphorisms)

One should never be sorry one has attempted something new—never, never, never.

—*Sybil Thorndike*
(after flopping in a
musical in 1962)

A daring beginning is halfway to winning.

—*Heinrich Heine*

Nothing comes of nothing.

—*William Shakespeare*

The beginning bears witness to the end, and the end will at long last bear witness to the beginning.

—*Leo Baeck*

Birthday

(also see AGING, BABY SHOWER / NEW BABY, COMING OF AGE)

Birthdays provide many quick and wonderful ways to bestow a quoted blessing, opinion, or jewel of wisdom on the celebrant. It can be done in a card, fax, or e-mail message; as part of a telephone or drop-by greeting; while giving a toast or testimonial at a birthday party; or on a simple slip of paper hidden inside a gift.

Birthdays also give the celebrant many golden opportunities to do his or her own bit of quoting. Indeed, it's a wise birthday boy, girl, man, or woman who keeps a couple of good quotes at tongue's tip just to avoid being caught speechless.

The selection below starts with a batch of general quotes, suitable for any age and focused on wishing happiness to the birthday celebrant. The remaining quotes relate to different, progressively older ages.

Believing hear, what you deserve to hear:
Your birthday as my own to me is dear . . .
But yours gives most; for mine did only lend
Me to the world; yours gave to me a friend.
                                    —*Martial* (Epigrams,
                                        bk. IX, epig. 52)

Do you count your birthdays thankfully?
                                    —*Horace* (Epistles)

Peace on your hand and health to all who shake it.
                                    —*Irish birthday blessing*

Where'er you walk cool gales shall fan the glade,
Trees where you sit shall crowd into a shade.
Where'er you tread the blushing flowers shall rise,
And all things flourish where you turn your eyes.
                                    —*Alexander Pope*
                                    ("Pastorals")

We are always the same age inside.
                                    —*Gertrude Stein*

May you live as long as you want, and never want as long as
you live.
                                    —*Irish birthday blessing*

When I was one-and-twenty
   I heard a wise man say,
"Give crowns and pounds and guineas
   But not your heart away;
Give pearls away and rubies
   But keep your fancy free."
But I was one and twenty,
   No use to talk to me.

When I was one-and-twenty
   I heard him say again,
"The heart out of the bosom
   Was never given in vain;
'Tis paid with sighs a-plenty
   And sold for endless rue."
And I am two-and-twenty,
   And oh, 'tis true, 'tis true.

               —*A.E. Housman*
               ("When I Was One-and-
               Twenty")

   The passions are the sails of the little ship, you know. And he who in his twentieth year gives way entirely to his feeling, catches too much wind and his boat ships too much water and—and he sinks—or comes to the surface again after all.
               —*Vincent Van Gogh*
               (letter, 1881)

   I'm six foot eleven. My birthday covers three days.
               —*Darryl Dawkins*

It takes about ten years to get used to how old you are.
                    —*Anonymous*

At thirty a man should know himself like the palm of his hand, know the exact number of his defects and qualities, know how far he can go, foretell his failures—above all accept these things.
                    —*Albert Camus* (Carnets)

If you haven't grown up by age 36, you don't have to.
                    —*James Gurney*

We grow neither better nor worse as we get old, but more like ourselves.
                    —*May Lamberton Becker*

Before your fortieth birthday keep circulating the story that you're thirty-nine. If people hear it often enough, they'll believe it for years.
                    —*Jack Benny*

At twenty years of age, the will reigns; at thirty, the wit; and at forty, the judgment. . . .
                    —*Benjamin Franklin*
                    (Poor Richard's Almanac)

It was only in my forties that I started feeling young.
                            —*Henry Miller*

I broke the back of life yesterday and started downhill toward old age. This fact has not produced any effect on me that I can detect.

                    —*Mark Twain*
                    (in a letter to his mother on
                    his forty-third birthday)

The man who views the world at 50 the same as he did at 20 has wasted 30 years of his life.
                            —*Muhammad Ali*

Forty is the old age of youth; fifty is the youth of old age.
                            —*Victor Hugo*

At fifty, everyone has the face he deserves.
                            —*George Orwell*
                            (Notebook, *1949*)

To me, old age is always fifteen years older than I am.
                            —*Bernard M. Baruch*

After a certain age, the more one becomes oneself, the more obvious one's family traits become.
                            —*Marcel Proust*

What a wonderful life I've had! I only wish I'd realized it sooner.

—*Colette*

Thomas Edison, the inventor, never minded his adult birthdays, for he knew the secret of staying young. Indeed, he was still inventing new things well into his eighth decade. In the 1920's, Henry Ford and Thomas Edison visited the California home of their mutual friend, Luther Burbank. Burbank kept a guest book where his visitors would sign in. Beside the name and address spaces was a space marked "interests." Ford watched Edison write in that space, "everything."

—*adapted from James C.*
Hume's Anecdotes
about the Famous

You can't help getting older, but you don't have to get old.

—*George Burns*

Age only matters when one is aging. Now that I have arrived at a great age, I might just as well be twenty.

—*Pablo Picasso*

When I was younger, I could remember anything, whether it had happened or not.

—*Mark Twain*

My birthday!—what a different sound
That word had in my youthful ears;
And now each time the day comes round
Less and less white its mark appears.

—*Thomas Moore*

Spring still makes spring in the mind
    When sixty years are told;
Love wakes anew this throbbing heart,
    And we are never old;

Over the winter glaciers
    I see the summer glow,
And through the wild-piled snow-drift
    The warm rosebuds below.

—*Ralph Waldo Emerson*
("We Are Never Old")

We will not speak of years tonight
    For what have years to bring
But larger floods of love and light
    And sweeter songs to sing?

—*Oliver Wendell Holmes*

Age I make light of it,
Fear not the sight of it,
Time's but our playmate, whose toys are divine.

—*Thomas Wentworth*
Higginson

Here I am, fifty-eight, and I still don't know what I'm going to be when I grow up.

—*Peter Drucker*

Beneath the moonlight and the snow
  Lies dead my latest year;
The winter winds are wailing low
  Its dirges in my ear.

I grieve not with the moaning wind
  As if a loss befell;
Before me, even as behind
  God is, and all is well.

Not mindless of the growing years
  Of care and loss and pain,
My eyes are wet with thankful tears
  For blessings which remain.

—*John Greenleaf Whittier*

I was asked the other day: "What are you doing nowadays?" "I'm busy growing older," I answered. "It's a whole-time job."

—*Paul Leautaud*
(Journal, *1907*)

No one is so old that he does not think he could live another year.

—*Cicero* (De Senectute, *a year before he died*)

I am getting to an age when I can only enjoy the last sport left. It is called hunting for your spectacles.

—*Lord Grey of Falloden*

Nobody grows old by merely living a number of years. People grow old only by deserting their ideals.

—*Samuel Ullman*

Old age is like a plane flying through a storm. Once you're aboard, there's nothing you can do.

—*Golda Meir*

You don't stop laughing because you grow old; you grow old because you stop laughing.

—*Michael Pritchard*

By the time you're eighty years old you've learned everything. You only have to remember it.

—*George Burns*

When one finds company in himself and his pursuits, he cannot feel old, no matter what his years may be.

—*A.B. Alcott*

Wrinkles should merely indicate where smiles have been.

—*Mark Twain*

Now, as I approach my eighty-fourth year—it seems even older when I see it in print—I find it interesting to reflect on what has made my life, even with its moments of pain, such an essentially happy one. I have come to the conclusion that the most important element in human life is faith. If God were to take away all His blessings: health, physical fitness, wealth, intelligence and leave me but one gift, I would ask for faith—for with faith in Him, in His goodness, mercy, love for me and belief in everlasting life, I believe I could suffer the loss of my other gifts, etc, and still be happy—trustful, leaving all to His Inscrutable Providence.

—*Rose Fitzgerald Kennedy*
(Times to Remember)

For the past eighty years I have started each day in the same manner. It is not a mechanical routine but something essential to my daily life. I go to the piano, and I play two preludes and fugues of Bach. I cannot think of doing otherwise. It is a sort of benediction on the house. But that is not its only meaning for me. It is a rediscovery of the world of which I have the joy of being a part. It fills me with awareness of the wonder of life, with a feeling of the incredible marvel of being a human being.

—*Pablo Casals*
(Joys and Sorrows)

Business/Work Occasions

(also see BEGINNING, LABOR DAY)

Business or work takes up the largest percentage of most people's waking lives. How unfortunate, therefore, that it is so often associated with the routine, the mundane, and the arduous!

With just a little effort and—in some cases—attitude adjustment, we can see that it actually involves many stirring roles, responsibilities, milestones, turning points, and accomplishments that deserve special words. And there are a number of possible occasions in the course of business or work life to do some of that motivational pointing, for example:

- a party to launch a new business, project, service, facility, or campaign;
- a ceremony to begin or end a fiscal year;
- an event honoring a special achievement, business anniversary, new employee, promotion, or retirement;
- an awards banquet, special seminar dinner, or convention kickoff;
- a luncheon or dinner for visiting clients, affiliates, or business associates;

- a speech at a public forum, sponsored event, or educational institution;
- a staff meeting, sales talk, office party, or gathering in the lounge.

For the most part, the quotes below can be applied directly or indirectly to almost any form of human endeavor: blue collar, white collar, or pink collar; professional or salaried; product- or service-oriented; public or private sector; corporate or freelance. They've been divided for convenience's sake into three groups:

1. PERSONAL ANECDOTES: humorous but thought-provoking glimpses into business or work lives.
2. PRACTICAL ADVICE: guidelines for business or work success.
3. BELIEFS AND MAXIMS: buisness or work-related creeds and values.

PERSONAL ANECDOTES

As far as I'm concerned, the best place in the world to be is on a good cutting horse working cattle.

—*Sandra Day O'Connor*

I was fired from my job at Howard Johnson's when somebody asked me the ice cream flavor of the week and I said, "Chicken."

—*Mike Nichols*

When I was six I made my mother a little hat—out of her new blouse.

>—*Lilly Dache*
>*(a hat designer)*

If Hollywood didn't work out, I was all prepared to be the best secretary in the world.

>—*Bette Davis*

I am a great believer in luck, and I find the harder I work the more I have of it.

>—*Stephen Leacock*

Adieu! I must now write to the king of France, compose a solo for flute, make up a poem for Voltaire, alter some army regulations, and do a thousand things!

>—*Frederick the Great of Prussia*
>*(in a letter to a friend just*
>*after his accession in 1740)*

Sometimes I worry about being a success in a mediocre world.

>—*Lily Tomlin*

PRACTICAL ADVICE

All the problems of the world could be settled easily if men were only willing to think. The trouble is that men very often resort to all sorts of devices in order not to think, because thinking is such hard work.

—*Thomas J. Watson*

Listen carefully to first criticisms made of your work. Note just what it is about your work that the critics don't like—then cultivate it. That's the only part of your work that's individual and worth keeping.

—*Jean Cocteau*

Always do one thing less than you think you can do.

—*Bernard Baruch*

One of the few things I know about writing is this: spend it all, shoot it, play it, lose it, all, right away, every time. Do not hoard what seems good for a later place in the book, or for another book; give it, give it all, give it now. The impulse to save something good for a better place later is the signal to spend it now. . . . Anything you do not give freely and abundantly becomes lost to you. You open your safe and find ashes.

—*Annie Dillard*
(A Writer's Life)

Measure twice . . . cut once.

—*Ross Perot*

My motto is first honesty, then industry, then concentration.

—*Andrew Carnegie*

The first step you should take if you want to be successful is to decide what kind of executive you are. Executives fall into three categories: Those who make things happen; those who watch things happen; and those who wonder what happened.
—*John M. Capozzi*

Next to knowing your own business, the best thing to know is all about the other fellow's business.
—*John D. Rockefeller*

Only through curiosity can we discover opportunities and only through gambling can we take advantage of them.
—*Clarence Birdseye*

Nothing succeeds like the appearance of success.
—*Christopher Lasch*

For peace of mind, resign as general manager of the universe.
—*Larry Eisenberg*

No great man ever complains of want of opportunity.
—*Ralph Waldo Emerson*

The shortest and best way to make your fortune is to let people see clearly that it is in their interests to promote yours.
—*Jean de La Bruyère*

No man ever listened himself out of a job.
                    —*Calvin Coolidge*

Be everywhere, do everything, and never fail to astonish the customer.
                    —*Margaret Getchell*

BELIEFS AND MAXIMS

In doing what we ought, we deserve no praise because it is our duty.
                    —*St. Augustine*
                    (Confessions)

Everyone entrusted with a mission is an angel.
                    —*Moses Maimonides*

In advertising there is a saying that if you can keep your head while all those around you are losing theirs—then you just don't understand the problem.
                    —*Hugh M. Beville, Jr.*

A committee is a group that keeps minutes and loses hours.
                    —*Milton Berle*

Good merchandise finds a ready buyer.
                    —*Plautus* (Paenulus)

Nowhere so busy a man as he there was,
And yet he seemed busier than he was.

> —*Geoffrey Chaucer*
> (Canterbury Tales,
> *Prologue)*

No phase of life, whether public or private, can be free from duty.

> —*Cicero* (De Officiis)

What I must do is all that concerns me, not what the people think.

> —*Ralph Waldo Emerson*
> (Self-Reliance)

God never imposes a duty without giving time to do it.

> —*John Ruskin* (Lectures on
> Architecture, *no. 2)*

Duty is what one expects from others.

> —*Oscar Wilde* (A Woman of
> No Importance, *Act. II)*

When the pace of change outside an organization becomes greater than the pace of change inside the organization, the end is near.

> —*John R. Walter*

Executive personalities can sometimes be measured by their actions. For example, in driving, there are two types of executive motorists—those who drive as if they owned the road, and those who drive as if they owned the car.

—*John M. Capozzi*

The playthings of our elders are called business.

—*St. Augustine*
(Confessions)

It's not the employer who pays the wages. Employers only handle the money. It's the customer who pays the wages.

—*Henry Ford*

If the spirit of business adventure is dulled, this country will cease to hold the foremost position in the world.

—*Andrew W. Mellon*

Success can eliminate as many options as failure.

—*Tom Robbins*

If you become a star, *you* don't change, everyone else does.

—*Kirk Douglas*

Going into business for yourself, becoming an entrepreneur, is the modern-day equivalent of pioneering on the old frontier.

—*Paula Nelson*

The chief business of the American people is business.
            —*Calvin Coolidge*

Whenever an individual or a business decides that success has been attained, progress stops.
            —*Thomas Watson*

In business, willingness is just as important as ability.
            —*Paul G. Hoffman*

The more people who own little businesses of their own, the safer our country will be, and the better off its cities and towns, for the people who have a stake in their country and their community are its best citizens.
            —*John Hancock*

The price of power is responsibility for the public good.
            —*Winthrop W. Aldrich*

There is no resting place for an enterprise in a competitive economy.
            —*Alfred P. Sloan*

No matter how far a person can go, the horizon is still way beyond you.
            —*Nora Zeale Hurston* (Their
                Eyes Were Watching God)

The hardest work in the world is being out of work.
—*Whitney Young, Jr.*

The confidence which we have in ourselves gives birth to much of that which we have in others.
—*François La Rochefoucauld*
(Premier Supplement)

It is not enough to be busy: so are the ants. The question is, What are we busy about?
—*Henry David Thoreau*

The future belongs to those who believe in the beauty of their dreams.
—*Eleanor Roosevelt*

Success in your work, the finding a better method, the better understanding that insures the better performing is hat and coat, is food and wine, is fire and horse and health and holiday. At least, I find that any success in my work has the effect on my spirits of all these.
—*Ralph Waldo Emerson*

Direct us, O Lord, in all our doings, with Thy most gracious favor, and further us with Thy continual help; that in all our works begun, continued, and ended in Thee, we may glorify Thy holy name, and finally, by Thy mercy, obtain everlasting life; through Jesus Christ our Lord, Amen.
—*Book of Common Prayer*

Christmas

(also see Winter)

The full Christmas season, honoring Christ's birth, stretches from the day after Thanksgiving, past Christmas Day on December 25, to Epiphany (also known as Twelfth Night or Three Kings Day) on January 6, making it the most expansive holiday season of the year. Nevertheless, the exchanging of greetings and singing of carols tend to end abruptly after December 25. That still leaves plenty of time to recite, read aloud, or write your favorite Christmas quotes!

The following assortment of quotations displays the wondrously varied elements that intermingle to give the holiday so much color and life: the sacred miracle of Christ's birth, the secular frenzy of gift buying, the quiet beauty of nature at rest, the fanciful folk images of Santa Claus and his reindeer, and the promise of new life to come in the faces of children and in the slowly lengthening hours of sunlight. Spread these words in your cards, during parties with friends, at the family table, and most especially, around the Christmas tree.

Joy to the World; the Lord is come;
Let Earth receive her King:
Let every Heart prepare him Room,
And Heaven and Nature sing.

—*Isaac Watts*

And it came to pass in those days that there went out a decree from Caesar Augustus, that all the world should be taxed. . . . And all went to be taxed, every one into his own city. And Joseph also went up from Galilee, out of the city of Nazareth, into Judaea, unto the city of David, which is called Bethlehem . . . to be taxed with Mary his espoused wife, being great with child. And so it was, that, while they were there, the days were accomplished that she should be delivered. And she brought forth her first-born son, and wrapped him in swaddling clothes, and laid him in a manger; because there was no room for them in the inn. And there were in the same country shepherds abiding in the field, keeping watch over their flock by night. And, lo, the angel of the Lord came upon them, and the glory of the Lord shone around them; and they were sore afraid. And the angel said unto them, Fear not: For behold, I bring you good tidings of great joy, which shall be to all people. For unto you is born this day in the city of David a Saviour, which is Christ the Lord. And this shall be a sign to you; Ye shall find the babe wrapped in swaddling clothes, lying in a manger. And suddenly there was with the angel a multitude of the heavenly host praising God, and saying, Glory to God in the highest, and on earth peace, good will toward men.

—*Bible, Luke 2:1–14*

A Christmas tree should be twice as tall as a boy, so a boy
can't steal the star.

　　　　　　　　　—*Truman Capote*
　　　　　　　　　(*a character in*
　　　　　　　　　A Christmas Memory)

'Twas the night before Christmas, when all through the house
Not a creature was stirring, not even a mouse;
The stockings were hung by the chimney with care,
In hopes that St. Nicholas soon would be there.
The children were nestled all snug in their beds,
While visions of sugar-plums danced in their heads;
And mamma in her 'kerchief, and I in my cap,
Had just settled our brains for a long winter's nap,
When out on the lawn there arose such a clatter,
I sprang from the bed to see what was the matter.
Away to the window I flew like a flash,
Tore open the shutters and threw up the sash.
The moon on the breast of the new-fallen snow,
Gave the luster of mid-day to objects below,
When, what to my wondering eyes should appear,
But a miniature sleigh, and eight tiny reindeer,
With a little old driver, so lively and quick,
I knew in a moment it must be St. Nick.
More rapid than eagles his coursers they came,
And he whistled, and shouted, and called them by name;
"Now, Dasher! now, Dancer! now, Prancer and Vixen!
On, Comet! on, Cupid! on, Donner and Blitzen!
To the top of the porch! to the top of the wall!
Now dash away! dash away! dash away all!"
As dry leaves that before the wild hurricane fly,
When they meet with an obstacle, mount to the sky,
So up to the house-top the coursers they flew,

With the sleigh full of toys and St. Nicholas too.
And then, in a twinkling, I heard on the roof
The prancing and pawing of each little hoof.
As I drew in my head, and was turning around,
Down the chimney St. Nicholas came with a bound.
He was dressed all in fur, from his head to his foot,
And his clothes were all tarnished with ashes and soot;
A bundle of toys he had flung on his back,
And he looked like a peddler just opening his pack.
His eyes—how they twinkled! his dimples how merry!
His cheeks were like roses, his nose like a cherry!
His droll little mouth was drawn up like a bow,
And the beard of his chin was as white as the snow.
The stump of a pipe he held tight in his teeth,
And the smoke it encircled his head like a wreath;
He had a broad face and a round little belly
That shook, when he laughed, like a bowl full of jelly.
He was chubby and plump, a right jolly old elf,
And I laughed when I saw him, in spite of myself;
A wink of his eye and a twist of his head,
Soon gave me to know I had nothing to dread;
He spoke not a word, but went straight to his work,
And filled all the stockings; then turned with a jerk,
And laying his finger aside of his nose,
And giving a nod, up the chimney he rose;
He sprang to his sleigh, to his team gave a whistle,
And away they all flew like the down on a thistle.
But I heard him exclaim, ere he drove out of sight,
"Happy Christmas to all, and to all a good night!"

—Clement C. Moore ("The Visit
of St. Nicholas")

Heap on more wood!—the wind is chill;
But let it whistle as it will,
We'll keep our Christmas merry still.

—Sir Walter Scott

Santa Claus has the right idea: Visit people once a year.

—Victor Borge

The pre-Christmas rush may do us greater service than we realize. With all its temporal confusion, it may just help us to see that by contrast, Christmas itself is eternal.

—Burton Hillis

Before the paling of the stars,
    Before the winter morn,
    Before the earliest cock-crow
Jesus Christ was born:
    Born in a stable,
    Cradled in a manger,
In the world His hands had made
    Born a stranger.

Priest and King lay fast asleep
    In Jerusalem,
Young and old lay fast asleep,
    In crowded Bethlehem:
Saint and angel, ox and ass,
    Kept a watch together,
    Before the Christmas daybreak
    In the winter weather.

Jesus on his Mother's breast
  In the stable cold,
Spotless Lamb of God was He,
  Shepherd of the fold:
Let us kneel with Mary Maid,
  With Joseph bent and hoary,
With Saint and Angel, ox and ass,
  To hail the King of Glory.

—*Christina Rossetti*

Folklore says that Martin Luther, the sixteenth-century Reformationist, is the father of the modern Christmas tree. As the story goes, Luther was trudging through the woods on a clear, cold Christmas Eve after having delivered a sermon at his church. Stopping in a grove of towering pine trees to admire the stars, he was struck by how much it looked as if the stars were actually hanging in the branches of the trees themselves. The fragrance of the trees seemed far finer than incense, and the soft sound made by their branches stirring in the wind suggested a devout congregation in prayer.

Inspired by this experience, he cut down a small pine tree and took it home with him. There he filled the branches with small candles, and told his children to imagine that the lit candles were stars in the sky on the night of Christ's birth. Thereafter, Luther's family had a Christmas tree each year, and the custom spread.

—*Jack Maguire*
(O, Christmas Tree!)

How many observe Christ's birthday! How few, his precepts! O! 'tis easier to keep holidays than commandments.

—*Ben Franklin*

Sing hey! Sing hey!
For Christmas Day;
Twine mistletoe and holly.
For a friendship glows
In winter snows,
And so let's all be jolly!

—*Anonymous*

Jesus our brother, strong and good,
Was humbly born in a stable rude,
And the friendly beasts around him stood
Jesus our brother, strong and good.

"I," said the donkey, shaggy and brown,
"I carried His mother up hill and down,
I carried her safely to Bethlehem town;
I," said the donkey, shaggy and brown.

"I," said the cow, all white and red,
"I gave Him my manger for His bed,
I gave Him my hay to pillow His head;
I," said the cow, all white and red.

"I," said the sheep, with curly horn,
"I gave Him my wool for His blanket warm,
He wore my coat on Christmas morn;
I," said the sheep, with curly horn.

"I," said the dove, from the rafters high,
"Cooed him to sleep, my mate and I;
We cooed him to sleep, my mate and I;
I," said the dove, from the rafters high.

And every beast, by some good spell,
In the stable dark was glad to tell,
Of the gift he gave Immanuel,
The gift he gave Immanuel.

—*Anonymous*

In 1897, a young girl named Virginia wrote a letter to the *New York Sun* asking if Santa Claus really did exist. Some of her friends, she stated, no longer believed in him. The reply was an editorial by Frank Church entitled, "Yes, Virginia, There Is A Santa Claus." It contained the following message: "Not believe in Santa Claus! You might as well not believe in fairies. . . . Nobody sees Santa Claus, but that is no sign there is no Santa Claus. The most real things in the world are those which neither children nor men can see. No Santa Claus! Thank God, he lives and he lives forever."

—*Jack Maguire*

I stopped believing in Santa Claus when I was six. Mother took me to see him in a department store and he asked for my autograph.

—*Shirley Temple*

I will honour Christmas in my heart, and try to keep it all the year!

—*Charles Dickens*

Coming of Age

❧

(also see BEGINNING, BIRTHDAY, COMMENCEMENT)

In recent years, increasing numbers of young people—ages 11 through 21—have been seeking more meaningful occasions to mark their transition from being a kid to becoming an adult. Parents, too, have been enthusiastically planning such events for their children. A coming-of-age ceremony helps ground the young person, giving him or her a keener sense of personal value and purpose in life. At the same time, it enables everyone around that young person to communicate love, regard, and best wishes for the future.

Sometimes a young person's coming-of-age celebration occurs in the context of an existing rite of passage: Christian youth can go through confirmation, or acceptance into the adult congregation. Judaism also offers confirmation or a more traditional bar mitzvah ceremony for a boy, and bas or bat mitzvah ceremony for a girl. Western culture in general provides high school or college commencement as a marking point. Other times, a young person has a more open-ended coming-of-age party that is custom-designed to celebrate just that.

Whatever the context or style, you can help make the coming-of-age ceremony more significant with your specially chosen words of wisdom. This is one occasion when it may be more appropriate to transfer those words into some kind of written form, so that the honoree can keep referring to them for inspiration or reality-checking.

————

The trick is growing up without growing old.
—*Casey Stengel*

A child becomes an adult when he realizes he has a right not only to be right but also to be wrong.
—*Thomas Szasz*
(The Second Sin)

I was a fourteen-year-old boy for thirty years.
—*Mickey Rooney*

Everything you are and do from fifteen to eighteen is what you are and will do through life.
—*F. Scott Fitzgerald (in a letter to his daughter, September 1938)*

Sad and terrible happenings had never made Frankie cry, but this season many things made Frankie suddenly wish to cry . . . home lights watched from the evening sidewalks, an unknown voice from an alley. She would stare at the lights and listen to the voice, and something inside her stiffened and waited. But the lights would darken, the voice fall silent, and though she waited that was all. She was afraid of these things that made her suddenly wonder who she was, and what she was going to be in the world, and why she was standing at that minute seeing a light, or listening, or staring up into the sky; alone.

—*Carson McCullers*
(*a character in* The Member of the Wedding)

When I was a child, I spake as a child, I understood as a child, I thought as a child; but when I became a man, I put away childish things.

—*Bible, I Corinthians*

I am an optimist. It does not seem too much use being anything else.

—*Sir Winston Churchill*

He was alone. He was unheeded, happy, and near to the wild heart of life. He was alone and young and willful and wild-hearted, alone amidst a waste of wild air and brackish waters and the sea harvest of shells and tangle and veiled grey sunlight.

—*James Joyce*

Happiness is not having what you want, but wanting what you have.

—*Rabbi Hyman Judah*
Schachtel

I think that a human being, a real artist, should set for himself the greatest goal. If you set for yourself a small goal you have already failed by the very fact that your goal is so small. Run as far as you can or at least try to. Never get tired. Never fall into despair. If you fall, begin again. That is what life is.

—*Isaac Bashevis Singer*

When a guru was asked, "What is the secret of life?," he answered, "Having good judgment."

"I see," said the seeker of wisdom. "And how does one acquire good judgment?"

The guru answered, "Through experience."

"I see," said the seeker. "And how do you obtain this experience?"

The guru smiled and replied, "Usually through bad judgment."

—*Indian parable (adapted from the* Storyteller's Calendar, *1994)*

The nearest way to glory is to strive to be what you wish to be thought to be.

—*Socrates*

A hero is simply someone who rises above his own human weaknesses, for an hour, a day, a year, to do something stirring.

—*Betty Deramus*

Heroes can be found less in large things than in small ones, less in public than in private.

—*James Baldwin* (Nobody Knows My Name)

In order to achieve any degree of success and happiness, use your senses wisely. Listen first and intently to what someone says and to what he isn't saying. Look with your eyes open, see the things that others don't see. Smell with the intent to recall the best feelings in your life, food, wine, and the air around you. Speak only when you have something that is important for someone else to hear, not simply because you wish to be heard. Touch everything around you; feel the joy of touching someone else's life as well as the friendship and warmth of a handshake. Use all your senses to enjoy your life to the fullest and to improve someone else's.

—*Wayne Kostroski*

And when he was twelve years old, they went up to Jerusalem after the custom of the feast.

And when they had fulfilled the days, as they returned, the child Jesus tarried behind in Jerusalem; and Joseph and his mother knew not of it.

But they, supposing him to have been in the company, went a day's journey; and they sought him among their kinsfolk and acquaintance.

And when they found him not, they turned back again to Jerusalem, seeking him.

And it came to pass, that after three days they found him in the temple, sitting in the midst of the doctors, both hearing them, and asking them questions.

And all that heard him were astonished at his understanding and his answers.

And when they saw him, they were amazed: and his mother said unto him, Son, why hast thou thus dealt with us? Behold, thy father and I have sought thee sorrowing.

And he said unto them, How is it that ye sought me? Wist ye not that I be in my father's house?

And they understood not the saying which he had spake unto them.

And he went down with them, and came to Nazareth, and was subject unto them: but his mother kept all these sayings in her heart.

And Jesus increased in wisdom and stature, and in favor with God and man.

—*Bible, Luke 2:42*

Experience is not what happens to you; it is what you do with what happens to you.

—*Aldous Huxley*

If you can keep your head when all about you
　　Are losing theirs and blaming it on you,
If you can trust yourself when all men doubt you,
　　But make allowance for their doubting too;
If you can wait and not be tired by waiting
　　Or being lied about don't deal in lies,
Or being hated don't give way to hating,
　　And yet don't look too good, nor talk too wise:

If you can dream—and not make dreams your master;
　　If you can think—and not make thoughts your aim,
If you can meet with Triumph and Disaster
　　And treat these two impostors just the same;
If you can bear to hear the truth you've spoken
　　Twisted by knaves to make a trap for fools,
Or watch the things you gave your life to, broken,
　　And stoop and build 'em up with worn-out tools:

If you can make one heap of all your winnings
　　And risk it on one turn of pitch-and-toss,

And lose, and start again at your beginnings
  And never breathe a word about your loss;
If you can force your heart and nerve and sinew
  To serve your turn long after they are gone,
And so hold on when there is nothing in you
  Except the will which says to them: "Hold on!"

If you can talk with crowds and keep your virtue,
  Or walk with Kings—nor lose the common touch,
If neither foes nor loving friends can hurt you,
  If all men count with you, but none too much;
If you can fill the unforgiving minute
  With sixty seconds' worth of distance run,
Yours is the Earth and everything that's in it,
  And—which is more—you'll be a Man, my son!
                    —*Rudyard Kipling ("If")*

Commencement

(also see Beginning, Coming of Age)

The word *commencement* applied to a ceremony usually refers to a high school graduation, college graduation, or the awarding of an advanced degree (Master or Doctor). It's an occasion for congratulatory cards, inspirational speeches, and parting words of advice—the best of all possible worlds for a quoter!

Life is something like this trumpet. If you don't put anything in it, you don't get anything out. And that's the truth.
> —W.C. Handy (early
> twentieth-century trumpeter
> and so-called Father of
> the Blues)

When you leave here, don't forget why you came.
> —Adlai Stevenson (to
> Princeton University
> graduates)

The ability to think straight, some knowledge of the past, some vision of the future, some skill to do useful service, some urge to fit that service into the well-being of the community—these are the most vital things education must try to produce.
—*Virginia Gildersleeve*

What sculpture is to a block of marble, education is to the soul.

—*Joseph Addison*
(The Spectator, *no. 215*)

Some of those young men make great and somewhat ridiculous efforts to stifle the contradictions they have felt rising within them or before them, without understanding that the spark of life can flash only between two contrary poles, and that it is larger and more beautiful the greater the distance between them and the richer the opposition with which each pole is charged.

—*André Gide*
(Journal, *1925*)

The roots of education are bitter, but the fruit is sweet.
—*Aristotle*

A smattering of everything, and a knowledge of nothing.
—*Charles Dickens* (Sketches by
Boz: *Sentiment*)

Too much and too little education hinder the mind.
—*Blaise Pascal* (Pensées, *sec.*
ii, no. 72)

There is a time in every man's education when he arrives at the conviction that envy is ignorance; that imitation is suicide; that he must take himself for better, for worse, as his portion; that though the wide universe is full of good, no kernel of nourishing corn comes to him but through his toil bestowed on that plot of ground which is given him to till. The power which resides in him is new in nature, and none but he knows what that is which he can do, nor does he know until he has tried.

—*Ralph Waldo Emerson*
(The American Scholar)

If you think education is expensive, wait till you see what ignorance costs you.

—*John M. Capozzi*

If you surrender to the wind, you can ride it.

—*Toni Morrison*

When all the fiercer passions cease
(The glory and disgrace of youth);
When the deluded soul, in peace,
Can listen to the voice of truth;
When we are taught in whom to trust,
And how to spare, to spend, to give,
(Our prudence kind, our pity just),
'Tis then we rightly learn to live.

—*George Crabbe*
(*"Reflection"*)

Nothing is worth more than this day.
>   —*Johann Wolfgang von*
>   *Goethe* (Maxims and
>   Reflections)

Capacities clamor to be used and cease their clamor only when they are well used.
>   —*Abraham Maslow*

. . . the idea that many people have that life is a vale of tears is just as false as the idea which the great majority have, and to which youth, health, and wealth incline you, that life is a place of entertainment. Life is a place of service, where one sometimes has occasion to put up with a lot that is hard, but more often to experience a great many joys.
>   —*Leo Tolstoy (in a letter to his*
>   *son, 1887)*

The man of imagination and no culture has wings without feet.
>   —*Joseph Joubert*

Pursue, keep up with, circle round and round your life, as a dog does his master's chaise. Do what you love. Know your own bone; gnaw at it, bury it, unearth it, and gnaw it still.
>   —*Henry David Thoreau*

A college education shows a man how little other people know.
>   —*Sam Slick*

When people are free to do as they please, they usually imitate each other.

—*Eric Hoffer*
(The Passionate State of
Mind)

I say, follow your bliss and don't be afraid, and doors will open where you didn't know they were going to be.

—*Joseph Campbell*

Hitch your wagon to a star.

—*Ralph Waldo Emerson*
(Society & Solitude)

Fare thee well;
The elements be kind to thee, and make
Thy spirits all of comfort!

—*William Shakespeare*
(Antony and Cleopatra,
Act III, sc. 2)

Easter

(also see Spring)

In A.D. 325, the Nicene Council decreed that Easter Sunday, the day commemorating Christ's resurrection three days after his crucifixion (Good Friday), would be the first Sunday after the full moon following the spring equinox. Thus, on a given year, Easter can occur anywhere between March 22 and April 25.

Whenever it comes, and whatever the weather, for Christians everywhere it's a day when spring in all its glory returns to the world and to the human spirit. It's a time to be humbled by God's sacrifice, generosity, and care, and yet to rejoice in the sheer wonder of life. Here are some quotes that are befitting both purposes.

Spring bursts today,
For Christ is risen and all the earth's at play.
>   —*Christina Rossetti*
>   *("Easter Carol")*

God expects from men . . . that their Easter devotions would in some measure come up to their Easter dress.

—*Robert Southey*

(Sermons, *vol. ii, no. 8)*

Then said our good Lord Jesus Christ: Art thou well pleased that I suffered for thee? I said: Yea, good Lord, I thank Thee: Yea, good Lord, blessed mayst thou be. Then said Jesus, our kind Lord: If thou art pleased, I am pleased: it is a joy, a bliss, an endless satisfying to me that ever suffered I Passion for thee; and if I might suffer more, I would suffer more.

Wherefore we be not only His by His buying, but also by the courteous gift of His Father, we be His bliss, we be His meed, we be His worship, we be His crown. (And this was a singular marvel and a full delectable beholding, that we be His crown!) This that I say is so great bliss to Jesus that He setteth at nought all His travail, and His hard Passion, and His cruel and shameful death.

—*Dame Julian of Norwich*

He is gone before thee, carrying His cross, and He died for thee upon the cross, that thou mayest also bear thy cross, and love to die on the cross. . . .

If thou carry the cross willingly, it will carry thee, and bring thee to thy desired end; to wit, to that place where there will be an end of suffering, though there will be no end here. . . .

Drink of the cup of the Lord lovingly, if thou desirest to be His friend, and to have part with Him.

Leave consolations to God to do with them as best it pleaseth Him.

But set thou thyself to bear tribulations, and account them the greatest consolations; for the sufferings of this life, although

thou alone couldst suffer them all, are not worthy to be com-
pared with the glory which shall hereafter be revealed in us.
                                        —*Thomas à Kempis*

O heart, be lifted up; O heart be gay,
Because the Light was lifted up to-day—
Was lifted on the Rood, but did not die,
To shine eternally for such as I.

O heart, rejoice with all your humble might
That God did kindle in the world this Light,
Which stretching on the Cross could not prevent
From shining with continuous intent.

Why weep, O heart, this day? Why grieve you so?
If all the glory of the Light had lost its glow
Would the sun shine or earth put on her best—
Her flower-entangled and embroidered vest?

Look up, O heart; and then, O heart, kneel down
In humble adoration: give no crown
Nor golden diadem to your fair Lord,
But offer love and beauty by your word.

Let your faith burn, O heart: and let your eyes
Shine with such joy where deepest night still lies
In some too tired and over-burdened mind:
Let Christ be seen, wherever you are kind.

O heart, let your light shine so that all men
May see your works and glorify again
Your Father: and oh! let your light be gay,
And full of quiet laughter all the day.

The everlasting fire of love, O heart,
Has blazed in you and it will not depart.
Wherefore, O heart, exult and praises sing:
Lift up your voice and make the echoes ring.

Raise up your hands, O heart: your fingers raise
In adoration; and in bursting praise
Sing all your songs of beauty with delight,
You larks, exulting in the summer light.

O heart, rise up: O heart be lifted high.
Rejoice; for Light was slain to-day, yet did not die.
                            —*Anonymous*

This is the promise that He hath promised us, even eternal
life.
                            —*Bible, I John 2:25*

Most glorious Lord of life, that on this day
    didst make thy triumph over death and sin:
    and having harrowed hell, didst bring away
    captivity thence captive us to win:
This joyous day, dear Lord, with joy begin,
    and grant that we for whom thou diddest die
    being with thy dear blood clean washed from sin,
    may live forever in felicity.
And that thy love we weighing worthily,
    may likewise love thee for the same again:
    and for thy sake that all like dead didst buy,
    with love may one another entertain.
So let us love, dear love, like as we ought,
    Love is the lesson which the Lord us taught.
                            —*Edmund Spenser*

Faith is the force of life.

—*Leo Tolstoy*
(My Confession)

Awake, thou wintry earth—
Fling off thy sadness!
Fair vernal flowers, laugh forth
Your ancient gladness!
Christ is risen.

—*Thomas Blackburn*

Tomb, thou shalt not hold Him longer;
Death is strong, but Life is stronger;
Stronger than the dark, the light;
Stronger than the wrong, the right;
Faith and Hope triumphant say
Christ will rise on Easter Day.

—*Phillips Brooks*

In the bonds of Death He lay
Who for our offense was slain;
But the Lord is risen today,
Christ hath brought us life again,
Wherefore let us all rejoice,
Singing loud, with cheerful voice,
Hallelujah!

—*Martin Luther*

Dating from Easter, life took on a newness which made it a
different kind of life not known before—life that will not be

content until all the world comes alive. Despair is death, and despair faded from the minds of men who believed. Fear is death, and fear no longer invaded the still hours. Cowardice is death, and cowardice ceased to be a part of those who knew Easter.

—Glenn H. Asquith

The one who gets a golden egg
Will plenty have and never beg.

The one who gets an egg of blue
Will find a sweetheart fond and true.

The one who gets an egg of white
In life shall find supreme delight.

A silver egg will bring much joy!
And happiness without alloy.

A lucky one—the egg of pink,
The owner ne'er sees danger's brink

The one who speckled egg obtains
Will go through life by country lanes.

*—sample of nineteenth-
century English Easter egg
fortunes*

Father's Day

On the calendar, Father's Day is the third Sunday in June—unofficially since 1910, and officially (by declaration of Congress) since 1972. But we're free to celebrate Dad whenever we want! And, of course, he's entitled to comment on his role and its special delights or burdens whenever *he* wants! Here are some words to help out or inspire both endeavors.

Father!—to God himself we cannot give a holier name.
—*William Wordsworth*

It is not flesh and blood but the heart which makes us fathers and sons.

—*Friedrich Schiller* (Die Rauber, *Act 1, sc. i*)

When I was a boy of fourteen, my father was so ignorant I could hardly stand to have the old man around. But when I got to be twenty-one, I was astonished at how much the old man had learned in those seven years.

—*Mark Twain*

What was silent in the father speaks in the son; and often I found the son the unveiled secret of the father.

—*Friedrich Nietzsche* (Thus
Spake Zarathustra)

The affection of a father and a son are different: the father loves the person of the son, and the son loves the memory of his father.

—*Anonymous*

My daddy's face is a study. Winter moves into it and presides there. His eyes become a cliff of snow threatening to avalanche, his eyebrows bend like black limbs of leafless trees. His skin takes on the pale cheerless yellow of winter sun; for a jaw he has the edges of a snowbound field dotted with stubble; his high forehead is the frozen sweep of the Erie.

—*Toni Morrison (a
character in "The Coming
of Maureen Peal")*

One father is more than a hundred schoolmasters.

—*George Herbert*

It behooves a father to be blameless if he expects his child to be.

—Homer

The words a father speaks to his children in the privacy of the home are not overheard at the time, but, as in whispering galleries, they will be clearly heard at the end and by posterity.

—Jean Paul Richter

A wise son maketh a glad father.

—Bible, Proverbs 10:1

Setting a good example for children takes all the fun out of middle age.

—William Faulkner

The most important thing my father did for me was exude a belief in himself, a confidence in himself that I knew I could not override.

—Oprah Winfrey

A father is a banker provided by nature.

—French proverb

No man is responsible for his father. That is entirely his mother's affair.

—Margaret Trumbull

I have found the best way to give advice to your children is to find out what they want and then advise them to do it.

—*Harry Truman*

O dearest, dearest boy! my heart
For better lore would seldom yearn,
Could I but teach the hundredth part
Of what from thee I learn.

—*William Wordsworth*

Fourth of July

(INDEPENDENCE DAY)

Since 1776, when the Continental Congress in Philadelphia declared its independence from England, the Fourth of July has been a day to celebrate life, liberty, and the pursuit of happiness! Just in case you're called or moved to speak or write on the occasion, here are words that ring out the message loud and clear.

———

We hold these truths to be self-evident, that all men are created equal, that they are endowed by their Creator with certain inalienable rights, that among these are life, liberty and the pursuit of happiness.

> —*Thomas Jefferson (near the beginning of the Declaration of Independence)*

The spirit of liberty is the spirit which is not too sure that it is right; the spirit which seeks to understand the minds of other men and women; the spirit which weighs their interests alongside its own without bias; the spirit of Him who, nearly two thousand years ago, taught mankind that lesson it has never learned, but has never quite forgotten—that there may be a Kingdom where the least shall be heard and considered side by side with the greatest.

—*Judge Learned Hand*

I celebrate myself, and sing myself,
And what I assume you shall assume,
For every atom belonging to me as good as belongs to you.
—*Walt Whitman*
("Song of Myself")

Works which endure come from the soul of the people. The mighty in their pride walk alone to destruction. The humble walk hand in hand with Providence to immortality. Their work survives. When the people of the Colonies were defending their liberties against the might of kings, they chose their banner from the design set in the firmament through all eternity. The flags of the great empires of that day are gone, but the Stars and Stripes remain. It pictures the vision of a people whose eyes were turned to the rising dawn. It represents the hope of a father for his posterity. It was never flaunted for the glory of royalty, but to be born under it is to be a child of a king and to establish a home under it is to be the founder of a royal house. . . . He who lives under it and is loyal to it is loyal to truth and justice everywhere.

—*Calvin Coolidge*

Our flag means all that our fathers meant in the
   Revolutionary War.
It means all that the Declaration of Independence meant.
It means justice.
It means liberty.
It means happiness.
Our flag carries American ideas, American history, and
   American feelings.
Every color means liberty.
Every thread means liberty.
Every star and stripe means liberty.
It does not mean lawlessness, but liberty through the law,
   and laws for liberty.
Forget not what it means.
And for the sake of its ideas, be true to your country's flag.
                                   —*Henry Ward Beecher*

Is life so dear, or peace so sweet, as to be purchased at the
price of chains and slavery? Forbid it, Almighty God! I know not
what course others may take, but as for me, give me liberty, or
give me death!
                                   —*Patrick Henry*

Democracy is cumbersome, slow, and inefficient, but in due
time, the voice of the people will be heard and their latent
wisdom will prevail.
                                   —*Thomas Jefferson*

The United States of America themselves are essentially the
greatest poem.
                                   —*Walt Whitman*
                                   (Leaves of Grass)

Hanukkah

The eight-day Hanukkah holiday for Jews begins on the twenty-fifth day of the Jewish month of Kislev—roughly around the time of the winter solstice. Historically, it honors the successful campaign in 164 B.C.E. of a band of Jews, led by Judah the Maccabee, against their Hellenic persecutors. Having finally liberated the temple in Jerusalem, the Maccabeans could locate only a day's worth of oil to burn. To their amazement, it burned for eight days—a miracle that's celebrated in the day-by-day lighting of the eight-branched menorah.

Another custom associated with Hanukkah is playing games of chance. For centuries, rabbis only allowed such games during this period because of its lengthy nights. By far the most popular one is spinning the dreidel, a top with a different Hebrew letter on each of its four sides (collectively forming an acronym for the phrase "A great miracle happened there").

It's also customary during Hanukkah to give gifts in honor of freedom from oppression and to eat fried potato pancakes (or latkes) to recall the oil burned in the temple.

The quotes below give you a range of appropriate sentiments to ponder—or share—at Hanukkah.

————

At Hanukkah, when we remember the battle for independence of the Jewish Maccabees against Syrian-Greek oppression, and when we recall how the oil light remained miraculously glowing for eight days in their outlawed and besieged temple, we rekindle our faith that God can give us more strength, more power, and more illumination than we can imagine, or than logic can explain.

—*Leon Golden*
(Children of Faith)

What's the best holiday? Hanukkah of course. . . . You eat pancakes every day, spin your dreidel to your heart's content, and from all sides money comes pouring in. What holiday can be better than that!

—*Sholom Aleichem*

Some symbols are so primary that purported "meanings" can only prove inadequate. Light in the dead of winter, victory when it had seemed improbable, more than enough when there had been far too little, few against many, the freedom to *be*—these are the essence, and the stories built around them only so much adornment. . . .

—*Arnold Eisen*

Traditionally, Hanukkah celebrates not a victory but a miracle. Although God may be present in all events, we sense God's presence in only those events in which there is an element of awe, and an element pointing to the hand of God. . . . Lest Hanukkah be overmilitarized, we should be cautious about describing what it is that we celebrate: the agency of God not only in our lives but in our history. For the Jews, history trails in the tracks of God.

—*Edward L. Greenstein*

Light gives of itself freely, filling all available space. It does not seek anything in return; it asks not whether you are friend or foe. It gives of itself and is not thereby diminished.

—*Michael Strassfeld*

Housewarming

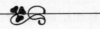

Many people throw their own housewarming party soon after moving into their new home. It's a way of making the place truly theirs in front of the world, whether they own it or not, and whether it's a room, apartment, condo, co-op, trailer, house, or mansion.

Other people leave it up to their family members and friends to "warm the house" on a one-by-one basis, as they drop by for their first visit.

Here's some ideal verbal kindling for doing that kind of warming!

If you're hosting your own party, you can use one or more of these quotes on an invitation. You can also post large sheets of paper with individual quotes around your new place, and invite your guests to bring their own quotes to post.

If you're visiting a new home for the first time, include a nicely printed quote with your gift, or simply recite it soon after you step across the threshold.

If you're not close enough to visit for a while, then send a quote. You'll arrive in spirit to bless the place!

———

'Mid pleasures and palaces though we may roam,
Be it ever so humble, there's no place like home.
A charm from the sky seems to hallow us there,
Which, seek through the world, is ne'er met with elsewhere.
Home! sweet home!
There's no place like home!

     —*John Howard Payne*

The ache for home lives in all of us, the safe place where we can go as we are and not be questioned.

     —*Maya Angelou*
     (All God's Children Need
     Traveling Shoes)

If I were asked to name the chief benefit of the house, I should say: the house shelters day-dreaming, the house protects the dreamer, the house allows one to dream in peace.

     —*Gaston Bachelard*

Home is the place you can go when you're whipped.

     —*Muhammad Ali*
     (The Greatest)

Home is a name, a word, it is a strong one; stronger than magician ever spoke, or spirit ever answered to, in the strongest conjuration.

     —*Charles Dickens*
     (Martin Chuzzlewit)

I live in my house as I live inside my skin: I know more beautiful, more ample, more sturdy and more picturesque skins: but it would seem to me unnatural to exchange them for mine.

—*Primo Levi*
("Other People's Trades")

If you want a golden rule that will fit everything, this is it: Have nothing in your houses that you do not know to be useful or believe to be beautiful.

—*William Morris*

Cleave to thine acre; the round year
Will fetch all fruits and virtues here.
Fool and foe may harmless roam,
Loved and lovers bide at home.

—*Ralph Waldo Emerson*

And the rain descended, and the floods came, and the winds blew, and beat upon that house; and it fell not: for it was founded upon a rock.

—*Bible, Matthew, 7:25*

He that has a house to put's head in has a good head-piece.

—*William Shakespeare*
(King Lear)

God bless the corners of this house
And be the lintel blessed.
Bless the hearth, the table too
And bless each place of rest.
Bless each door that opens wide
To stranger, kith, and kin;
Bless each shining window-pane
That lets the sunshine in.
Bless the roof-tree up above.
Bless every solid wall.
The peace of man, the peace of love,
The peace of God on all.

—Anonymous

May the roof above us never fall in
And may we good companions beneath it never fall out.

—Irish blessing

Where thou art—that—is Home.

—Emily Dickinson

Stay, stay at home, my heart, and rest;
Home-keeping hearts are happiest.

*—Henry Wadsworth
Longfellow*

It takes hands to build a house, but only hearts can build a home.

—Anonymous

Labor Day

(also see BUSINESS/WORK OCCASIONS)

In May, 1882, Peter J. McGuire, president of the United Brotherhood of Carpenters and Joiners of America, proposed to the New York Central Labor Union that there be a special "Labor Day" holiday for workers on the first Monday in September, roughly halfway between the Fourth of July and Thanksgiving. Understandably, every worker who heard about the idea loved it! Over the next fifty years, Labor Day became institutionalized across the country.

Let's hear it for workers!

I hear America singing, the varied carols I hear,
Those of mechanics, each one singing his as it should be
    blithe and strong,
The carpenter singing as he measures his plank or beam,
The mason singing his as he makes ready for work, or leaves
    off work,

The boatman singing what belongs to him in his boat, the
    deckhand singing on the steamboat deck,
The shoemaker singing as he sits on his bench, the hatter
    singing as he stands,
The wood-cutter's song, the ploughboy's on his way in the
    morning, or at noon intermission or at sundown,
The delicious singing of the mother, or of the young wife at
    work, or of the girl sewing or washing,
Each singing what belongs to him or her and to none else,
The day what belongs to the day—at night the party of
    young fellows, robust, friendly,
Singing with open mouths their strong melodious songs.

                —Walt Whitman
               (Leaves of Grass)

To labor is to pray.

              —Motto of the Benedictines

No man is born into the world whose work
Is not born with him; there is always work
And tools to work withal, for those who will;
And blessed are the horny hands of toil;
    The busy world shoves angrily aside
The man who stands with arms akimbo set,
Until occasion tells him what to do;
And he who waits to have his task marked out,
Shall die and leave his errand unfulfilled.

              —James Russell Lowell

Work banishes those three great evils: boredom, vice, and poverty.

—*Voltaire*

You are demanding that this city [Memphis] respect the dignity of labor. So often we overlook the work and the significance of those who are not in professional jobs, of those who are not in so-called big jobs. Let me say to you, whenever you are engaged in work that serves humanity and is for the building of humanity, it has dignity, it has worth.

—*Martin Luther King, Jr.*
(speech to sanitation workers,
Memphis, TN, April 3, 1968)

Skilled work, of no matter what kind, is only done well by those who take a certain pleasure in it, quite apart from its utility, either to themselves in earning a living, or to the world through its outcome.

—*Bertrand Russell*

I like work; it fascinates me. I can sit and look at it for hours. I love to keep it by me: the idea of getting rid of it nearly breaks my heart.

—*Jerome K. Jerome*

Martin Luther King, Jr., Day

❦❧

Born in Atlanta, Georgia, on January 15, 1929, Martin Luther King, Jr., became nationally recognized as a leader in the civil rights movement in 1963, after organizing a nonviolent protest campaign against segregation in Birmingham, Alabama. On August 28 of that year, he delivered his famous "I Have a Dream" speech to more than 200,000 participants in the "March on Washington [D.C.]" for racial equality. The following year, he received the Nobel Peace Prize. He was assassinated on April 4, 1968, in Memphis, Tennessee, where he'd come to participate in a strike-for-rights of the city's sanitation workers.

King's birthday was declared a federal holiday in 1983. On this day, ponder his stirring statements and the tributes of people who followed his vision; and, if the opportunity presents itself, convey some of these words to others.

I have a dream that one day this nation will rise up and live out the true meaning of its creed: "We hold these truths to be self-evident, that all men are created equal."

I have a dream that one day . . . sons of former slaves and sons of former slave-owners will be able to sit down together at the table of brotherhood. . . .

I have a dream that . . . little children will one day live in a nation where they will not be judged by the color of their skin but by the content of their character.

I have a dream that one day . . . little black boys and black girls will be able to join hands with little white boys and white girls as brothers and sisters.

—Martin Luther King, Jr.
(speech at the March on
Washington, August 28,
1963)

America is essentially a dream, a dream as yet unfulfilled. It is a dream of a land where men of all races, of all nationalities and of all creeds can live together as brothers.

—Martin Luther King, Jr.
(speech at Lincoln University,
Oxford, PA, June 6, 1961)

Until that moment comes when we, the Americans, are able to accept the fact that our ancestors are black and white, that on that continent we are trying to forge a new identity, that we need each other, that I am not a ward of America, I am not an object of missionary, I am one of the people who built this country . . . there is scarcely any hope for the American Dream. If they are denied participation in it, by their very presence they will wreck it.

—James Baldwin (speech in
Cambridge, England, 1965)

He was The One, The Hero, The One Fearless Person for whom we had waited. I hadn't even realized before that we *had* been waiting for Martin Luther King, Jr., but we had. And I knew it for sure when my mother added his name to the list of people she prayed for every night.

—Alice Walker (In Search of
Our Mothers' Garden)

Say . . . that I tried to love and serve humanity. . . . [S]ay that I was a drum major for peace . . . for righteousness.

—Martin Luther King, Jr.
(shortly before his
assassination)

Memorial Day

(Decoration Day; also see VETERANS DAY)

Now observed on the last Monday in May, Memorial Day was established by the U.S. Congress on May 30, 1868 to honor U.S. soldiers who died in the Civil War. Specifically, it was a day to decorate their graves with flowers. States that had belonged to the Confederacy already had special memorial days for their war heroes, so in the South this day was—and still is—commonly called Decoration Day to distinguish it.

Over the years Memorial Day has become a time to honor men and women who have given their lives in *all* armed conflicts fought by U.S. forces, not just those who perished in the Civil War. The quotations here include many of the most beautiful ways these valiant people have been remembered.

Fourscore and seven years ago our fathers brought forth on this continent a new nation, conceived in liberty and dedicated to the proposition that all men are created equal. Now we are engaged in a great civil war, testing whether that nation, or any nation so conceived and so dedicated, can long endure. We are met on a great battlefield of that war. We have come to dedicate a portion of that field as a final resting place for those who here gave their lives that that nation might live. It is altogether fitting and proper that we should do this. But, in a larger sense, we cannot dedicate—we cannot consecrate—we cannot hallow—this ground. The brave men, living and dead, who struggled here have consecrated it far above our poor power to add or to detract. The world will little note nor long remember what we say here, but it can never forget what they did here. It is for us, the living, rather to be dedicated here to the unfinished work which they who fought here have thus far so nobly advanced. It is rather for us to be here dedicated to the great task remaining before us—that from these honored dead we take increased devotion to that cause for which they gave the last full measure of devotion; that we here highly resolve that these dead shall not have died in vain; that this nation, under God, shall have a new birth of freedom; and that government of the people, by the people, for the people, shall not perish from the earth.

—*Abraham Lincoln*
("The Gettysburg Address")

Oh, tell me not that they are dead—that generous host, that airy army of invisible heroes! They hover as a crowd of witnesses above this nation. Are they dead that yet speak louder than we speak, and a more universal language? Are they dead that yet act? Are they dead that yet move upon society, and inspire the people with nobler motives and more heroic patriotism?

Every mountain and hill shall have its treasured name, every river shall keep some solemn title, every valley and every lake shall cherish its honest register; and till the mountains are worn out, and the rivers forget to flow—till the clouds are weary of replenishing springs, and the springs forget to gush, and the rills to sing, shall their names be kept fresh with reverent honors which are inscribed upon the book of national remembrance!

—*Henry Ward Beecher*

Who goes there, in the night,
  Across the storm-swept plain?
We are the ghosts of a valiant war—
  A million murdered men!

Who goes there, at the dawn,
  Across the sun-swept plain?
We are the ghosts of those who swear;
  It shall not be again!

—*Thomas Curtis Clark*

Almighty God, who hast given us this good land for our heritage; we humbly beseech Thee that we may always prove ourselves a people mindful of Thy favor and glad to do Thy will. Bless our land with honorable industry, sound learning, and pure manners. Save us from violence, discord, and confusion; from pride and arrogancy, and from every evil way. Defend our liberties, and fashion into one united people the multitudes brought hither out of many kindreds and tongues. Embue with the spirit of wisdom those to whom in Thy name we entrust the authority of government, that there may be justice and peace at home, and that, through obedience to Thy law, we may show forth Thy praise among the nations of the earth. In the time of prosperity, fill our hearts with thankfulness, and in the day of trouble, suffer not our trust in Thee to fail; all which we ask through Jesus Christ our Lord. Amen.

—Book of Common Prayer

Then strew bright flow'rs on ev'ry grave
    Wherein a hero lies,
And let the dear old banner wave
    'Neath freedom's sunlit skies.

The first clear notes the bugle blew,
    Were special calls to them,
And with their country's weal in view
    They went forth strong, armed men.
Left fathers, mothers, sisters, wives,
    And children young and pure,
And held as naught their precious lives,
    That homes might still endure.

To them be honor, earnest, true,
    And may we ne'er forget:
They died for me, they died for you,
    Where hostile armies met.
Come, lay upon each grassy bed
    A garland rich and rare,
Wherever sleep our soldier dead,
    Let them this tribute share.

—Anonymous

Eternal God, Father of all souls, grant unto us such clear vision of the sin of war, such hearty hatred for the passions which create it and for the desolations which follow it, that we may earnestly desire and tirelessly seek that co-operation between nations which alone can make war impossible. . . . Break down all race prejudice, all ignoble narrowness in national loyalty; stay the greed of those who profit by war and the ambitions of those who by imperialistic conquest seek a national greatness which, drenched in blood, cannot endure . . . ; arouse in the whole body of the people an adventurous willingness, as they sacrificed greatly for war, as also for international goodwill to dare bravely, to think wisely, to decide resolutely, and to achieve triumphantly.

—*Harry Emerson Fosdick*

Memorial Service

(or Funeral)

When death strikes a family member, friend, or acquaintance—
or when we commemorate that death in years to come—it's a
blessing to have suitable words available to ease the pain of the
survivors, pay proper respect to the deceased, and resolve one's
own feelings of sorrow and mortality. This category, Memorial
Service, contains a wide variety of quotations that address these
various needs. They are especially appropriate to speak, write,
or contemplate at the time of a wake, funeral, burial service, or
any kind of memorial service.

The entries are organized into four general groups as follows:

1. REMEMBERING THE DEAD: quotes that refer directly or indirectly to the deceased.
2. DEATH AND DYING: quotes about what it means to face death
   or die.
3. THE MOURNING PROCESS: quotes about coping with grief and
   bereavement.
4. PERSONAL THOUGHTS: quotes offering different individual per-
   spectives on death.

REMEMBERING THE DEAD

These quotes allude to the deceased in various ways—some very generally, others more specifically. If you wish, you can use one of these quotes as a springboard to offering remarks of your own that are more descriptive of the individual(s) being memorialized.

Two fairly specialized quotes deserve some explanation. The one by Sir Henry Worton refers to a wife who dies soon after losing her husband, a frequent occurrence among very close, long-term couples. The one by Percy Bysshe Shelley is appropriate to use in the case of two closely associated people (spouses, inseparable friends, or family members living together) who die at the same time and are buried together.

———

The life of the dead is placed in the memory of the living.
—*Cicero* (Philippicae)

Is there not a certain satisfaction in the fact that natural limits are set to the life of an individual, so that at its conclusion it may appear as a work of art?
—*Albert Einstein*

A human life is a story told by God.
—*Hans Christian Andersen*

Cowards die many times before their deaths;
The valiant never taste of death but once.
—*William Shakespeare*
(Julius Caesar)

And with the morn those angel faces smile
Which I have loved long since and lost awhile.
—*John Henry Newman*

He kept at true good humour's mark
The social flow of pleasure's tide:
He never made a brow look dark,
Nor caused a tear, but when he died.
—*Thomas Love Peacock*
("Headlong Hall: Song")

When he shall die
Take him and cut him out in little stars
And he will make the face of heav'n so fine
That all the world will be in love with night
And pay no worship to the garish sun.
—*William Shakespeare*
(Romeo and Juliet)

There are stars whose radiance is visible on earth though they have long been extinct. There are people whose brilliance continues to light the world though they are no longer among the living. These lights are particularly bright when the night is dark.

—*Hannah Senesch*

He first deceas'd; She for a little tri'd
To live without him: lik'd it not, and di'd.
—*Sir Henry Worton*

These are two friends whose lives were undivided;
So let their memory be, now they have glided
Under the grave; let not their bones be parted,
For their two hearts in life were single-hearted.

—*Percy Bysshe Shelley*
("Epitaph")

He who has gone, so we but cherish his memory, abides with us, more potent, nay, more present than the living man.

—*Antoine de Saint-Exupéry*

One cannot live with the dead; either we die with them or we make them live again. Or else we forget them.

—*Louis Martin-Chauffier*

The deep pain that is felt at the death of every friendly soul arises from the feeling that there is in every individual something which is inexpressible, peculiar to him alone, and is, therefore, absolutely and *irretrievably* lost.

—*Arthur Schopenhauer*

What the heart has once owned and had, it shall never lose.

—*Henry Ward Beecher*

The holiest of all holidays are those kept by ourselves in silence and apart, the secret anniversaries of the heart, when the full tide of feeling overflows.

—*Henry Wadsworth Longfellow*

DEATH AND DYING

These quotes ponder the awesome mystery of death. Being somewhat more neutral and soothing in tone than the other quotes, they're appropriate to express when you want to shift the focus, if only temporarily, beyond the actual deceased person or the manner in which he or she died to the general subject of death itself.

———

We must needs die, and are as water spilt on the ground, which cannot be gathered up again.
> —*Bible, 2 Samuel 14:14*

The hour which gives us life begins to take it away.
> —*Seneca*

What is this death?—a quiet of the heart?
The whole of that of which we are a part?
> —*George Gordon, Lord*
> *Byron* (Don Juan)

Death, like birth, is a secret of Nature.
> —*Marcus Aurelius*
> (Meditations, *book IV*)

Even at our birth, death does but stand aside a little. And every day he looks toward us and muses somewhat to himself whether that day or the next he will draw nigh.

—*Robert Bolt* (A Man For
All Seasons)

All goes onward and outward, nothing collapses,
And to die is different from what any one supposed, and
    luckier.

—*Walt Whitman*
(Leaves of Grass)

The last day does not bring extinction, but change of place.

—*Cicero* (Tusculanarum
Disputationum)

Thus shall ye think of all this fleeting world
A star at dawn, a bubble in a stream,
A flash of lightning in a summer cloud,
A flickering lamp, a phantom, and a dream.

—*from the Diamond Sutra*

All his earthly past will have been heaven to those who are saved. . . . The good man's past begins to change so that his forgiven sins and remembered sorrows take on the quality of heaven. . . . At the end of all things, the blessed will say, "We never lived anywhere but in heaven."

—*C.S. Lewis*

Death be not proud, though some have called thee
Mighty and dreadful, for thou art not so:
For those whom thou thinks't thou dost overthrow
Die not, poor Death; nor yet canst thou kill me.
From Rest and Sleep, which but thy picture be,
Much pleasure, then from thee much more must flow;
And soonest our best men with thee do go—
Rest of their bones and souls' delivery!
Thou'rt slave to fate, chance, kings, and desperate men,
And dost with poison, war, and sickness dwell;
And poppy or charms can make us sleep as well
And better than thy stroke. Why swell'st thou then?
One short sleep past, we wake eternally,
And death shall be no more: Death, thou shalt die!
                                    —*John Donne*

Man is like a breath, his days are like a passing shadow.
. . . So teach us to treasure our days that we may get a wise
heart.
                          —*Bible, Psalms 144:4, 90:12*

The day of death is when two worlds meet with a kiss: This
world going out, the future world coming in.
                                    —*Talmud*

God himself took a day to rest in, and a good man's grave is
his Sabbath.
                                    —*John Donne*

Sustained and soothed
By an unfaltering trust, approach thy grave,
Like one who wraps the drapery of his couch
About him, and lies down to pleasant dreams.
—*William Cullen Bryant*
(*"Thanatopsis"*)

May heaven be your bed!
—*Irish blessing*

THE MOURNING PROCESS

The following quotes, like prayers in general, are designed to
help survivors cope with their feelings of grief and bereavement.

Blessed are they that mourn, for they shall be comforted.
—*Bible, Matthew 5:4*

Let not the eyes be dry when we have lost a friend, nor let
them overflow. We may weep, but we must not wail.
—*Seneca* (Epistulae ad
Lucilium)

When you gaze upon the dead, remember this: You have
been shown more than you can understand.
Search not for what has been hidden from you. Seek not to
comprehend what is difficult to bear. Be not preoccupied with
what is beyond your ken.
Mourn the dead, yes. Hide not your grief. Restrain not your

sorrow or your lamentations. But remember: Suffering without end is worse than death.

Fear not death, for we are all destined to die. Fear not death, for we share it with all who ever lived and with all who ever will be.

The dead are at rest. Let the pangs of memory rest, too.

As a drop of water in the immensity of the sea, as a grain of sand on the measureless shore, so are man's few days in the light of eternity.

O God, our Father, You redeem our souls from the grave. Forsake us not in the days of our distress and desolation. Help us to live on, for we have placed our hope in Thee.

—ben Sirach (adapting
Ecclesiasticus)

Despair not only aggravates our misery, but our weakness.
—Henry David Thoreau
(Walden)

Grant that we here before Thee may be set free from the fear of vicissitude and from the fear of death, may finish what remains before us of our course without dishonor to ourselves, or hurt to others and, when the day comes, may die in peace. Deliver us from fear and favor, from mean hopes and cheap pleasures. Have mercy on each in his deficiency, let him not be cast down. Support the stumbling on the way and give at last rest to the weary. Amen.

—Robert Louis Stevenson

Though I walk through the valley of the shadow of death, I will fear no evil; for you are with me.
—Bible, Psalm 23

PERSONAL THOUGHTS

These quotes represent a spectrum of highly personal responses to death that are interesting—and sometimes helpful—to ponder. A particular quote may not be suitable to share with some mourners; but with others, it may be just what they need to hear, either because it reminds them happily of the deceased person, or clarifies their own nagging thoughts.

Every day, and all day long, I ask myself this question—or rather this question asks itself of me: Shall I find it hard to die? I do not think that death is particularly hard for those who most loved life. On the contrary.

—André Gide
(Journal, 1922)

Gaily I lived as ease and nature taught,
And spent my little life without a thought,
And am amazed that Death, that tyrant grim,
Should think of me, who never thought of him.

—René François Regnier
("Epigram")

We rejoice over a birth and mourn over a death. But we should not. For when a man is born, who knows what he will do or how he will end? But when a man dies, we may rejoice—if he left a good name and this world is in peace.

—adapted from Midrash:
Tanhuman on Exodus

What we call mourning for our dead is perhaps not so much grief at not being able to call them back as it is grief at not being able to want to do so.

—*Thomas Mann*
(The Magic Mountain)

The only way we can really achieve freedom is to somehow conquer the fear of death. For if a man has not discovered something that he will die for he isn't fit to live.

—*Martin Luther King, Jr.*

I decided that I would make my life my argument. I would advocate the things I believed in terms of the life I lived and what I did.

—*Albert Schweitzer (on how to respond to the inevitability of death)*

Who dares say no when the Angel of Death calls? You can be in your grocery store ringing up a hundred-dollar sale on the cash register and Death will call and you'll have to drop the sale and go. You can be riding around in your Buick and Death will call and you'll have to go. You are about to get out of your bed to go down to your job and old Death will call and you'll have to go. Mebbe [sic] you are building a house and called the mason and the carpenter and then Death calls and you have to go. Death's asking you to come to your last home.

—*Richard Wright*
(*a character in* The Long Dream)

People do not die for us immediately, but remain bathed in a sort of aura of life which bears no relation to true immortality but through which they continue to occupy our thoughts in the same way as when they were alive. It is as though they were traveling abroad.

—*Marcel Proust*
(Remembrance of
Things Past)

I imagine death to be like sleep. When death comes to you, you just pass out, just the way you passed out last night.

—*Ray Charles* (Brother Ray)

I am not going to die, I'm going home like a shooting star.

—*Sojourner Truth*

Mother's Day

Since 1914, the second Sunday in May has officially been Mother's Day, thanks to President Woodrow Wilson (and, by extension, his mother). But how do you pay tribute to someone whose love goes so far beyond words?

Here the children themselves do most of the talking! You can either quote their reminiscences at a Mother's Day gathering, or use them as models for your own. Better yet, why not do both?

God could not be everywhere, so he created mothers.
—Jewish saying

Strength and honour are her clothing;
    and she shall rejoice in time to come.
She openeth her mouth with wisdom;
    and in her tongue is the law of kindness.
She looketh well to the ways of her household,
    and eateth not the bread of idleness.

Her children rise up and call her blessed;
  her husband also, and he praiseth her.
Many daughters have done virtuously,
  but thou excellest them all.

—*Bible, Proverb 31*

What mother sings to the cradle goes all the way down to the coffin.

—*Henry Ward Beecher*
(Proverbs from Plymouth
Pulpit)

I always wondered about where "kingdom come" might be, since my mother threatened so many times to knock me there.
—*Bill Cosby*

I feel about mothers the way I feel about dimples: because I do not have one myself, I notice everyone who does. Most people who have a dimple or two take them for granted . . . while I spent months of my childhood going to bed with a button taped into each cheek trying to imprint nature. . . . Most people who have a mother take her for granted in much the same way. . . . Since I lost my mother when I was quite young, I keep pressing my mother-memories into my mind, like the buttons in my cheeks, hoping to deepen an imprint that time has tried to erase.

—*Letty Cottin Pogrebin*

Momma was home. She was the most totally human, human being that I have ever known; and so very beautiful. She was the lighthouse of her community. Within our home, she was an abundance of love, discipline, fun, affection, strength, tenderness, encouragement, understanding, inspiration, support.

—*Leontyne Price*

Who ran to help me when I fell,
And would some pretty story tell,
Or kiss the place to make it well?
My Mother.

—*Ann Taylor*

Mama was my greatest teacher, a teacher of compassion, love, and fearlessness. If love is sweet as a flower, then my mother is that sweet flower of love.

—*Stevie Wonder*

When a cake was in the oven an aura of mystery fell over the house. The shades were drawn, windows shut, neighbors informed. Mama moved cautiously about in house slippers. She knew nothing about thermodynamics. She knew only that a sponge cake is supposed to rise slowly and that the slightest sneeze within an area of twenty miles could cause a collapse. I would come home from school, slam the door, and hear a horrible scream from the kitchen: "Murderer! You killed my cake!"

—*Sam Levenson* (In One Era
and Out the Other)

The sweetest sounds to mortals given
Are heard in Mother, Home, and Heaven.
> —*William Goldsmith Brown*

Whenever a child is born, and the old miracle of motherhood with all its heroism and love is enacted afresh, there the angels' choir chant anew the sweet tidings of glory and peace and good will.
> —*Hyman G. Enelow*

My mother loved children—she would have given anything if I had been one.
> —*Groucho Marx*

There is no place I'd rather be tonight, except in my mother's arms.
> —*Duke Ellington (speech given at the White House, 1969)*

When my kids become wild and unruly, I use a nice, safe playpen. When they're finished, I climb out.
> —*Erma Bombeck*

The mother's heart is the child's schoolroom.
> —*Henry Ward Beecher*

Don't aim to be an earthly Saint, with eyes fixed on a star,
Just try to be the fellow that your Mother thinks you are.
> —*Will S. Adkin*

You may have tangible wealth untold;
Caskets of jewels and coffers of gold.
Richer than I you can never be—
I had a mother who read to me.
                              —*Strickland Gillilan*

No matter how old a mother is, she watches her middle-aged children for signs of improvement.
                              —*Florida Scott-Maxwell*

A mother's love endures through all; in good repute, in bad repute, in the face of the world's condemnation, a mother still loves on, and still hopes that her child may turn from his evil ways, and repent; she . . . remembers the infant smiles . . . the joyful shout of childhood . . . the promise of his youth; and she can never be brought to think him all unworthy.
                              —*Washington Irving*

Biology is the least of what makes someone a mother.
                              —*Oprah Winfrey*

The hand that rocks the cradle . . . rules the world.
                              —*William Ross Wallace*

New Year's Eve/Day

(also see BEGINNING)

Here's an assortment of timeless quotations to use when send-ing seasonal cards to friends and family members, when toast-ing, boasting, or coasting your way through a New Year's cele-bration, or when first greeting people in the new year.

Ring out the old, ring in the new,
  Ring, happy bells, across the snow:
  The year is going, let him go;
Ring out the false, ring in the true.
                    —*Alfred, Lord Tennyson*

Year's end is neither an end nor a beginning but a going on,
with all the wisdom that experience can instill in us.
                    —*Hal Borland*

The year hastens to its close. What is it to me? What I am, that is all that affects me. That I am twenty-eight or eight or fifty-eight years old is as nothing. Should I mourn that the spring flowers are gone, that the summer fruit has ripened, that the harvest is reaped, that the snow has fallen?

—Ralph Waldo Emerson
(Journal, *New Year's Day,*
1831)

Plant carrots in January and you'll never have to eat carrots.
—Anonymous

Never tell your resolution beforehand, or it's twice as onerous a duty.
—John Selden

Drop the last year into the silent limbo of the past. Let it go, for it was imperfect, and thank God that it can go.
—Brooks Atkinson

Always bear in mind that your own resolution to succeed is more than any other one thing.
—Abraham Lincoln

What better wish can be given you than that in the coming year you may never lose an old friend, but gain many new; that you may never do an unkindness, for which you would be sorry; that while God's sunshine is upon you, then will not be forgotten the blessing of it; that when clouds arrive, you will think with joy of the possibility of sunshine; and that on the gay opening of the year, you will remember:

"If all the year were playing holidays,
To sport would be as tedious as to work."
                                        —Anonymous

If you have tried to do something but couldn't, you are far better off than if you had tried to do nothing and succeeded.
                                        —John T. Ragland, Jr.

Passover

(*PESACH*)

Passover (or Pesach) is the Jewish festival from the fifteenth to the twenty-first of Nisan (in March or April) commemorating the flight of the Hebrews from slavery in ancient Egypt. The term comes from the fact that the Angel of Death, sent by God to kill the eldest son in every Egyptian family, "passed over" Hebrew households. The Hebrews subsequently ran away from Egypt in such haste that they made bread only with water and wheat baked in the sun, rather than waiting for leavened (yeast-risen) bread. The main feature of the Passover celebration is a Seder, a feast whose ritual structure features readings from the Haggadah. The quotations below include a passage from this book.

Ye shall observe the feast of unleavened bread.
—*Bible, Exodus 12:17*

Passover affirms the great truth that liberty is the inalienable right of every human being.

—*Max Joseph*

The Seder nights . . . tie me with the centuries before me.

—*Ludwig Frank*

The Exodus from Egypt occurs in every human being, in every era, in every year, and even in every day.

—*Rabbi Nachman of Bratislava*

Whoever has not said the verses concerning the following three things at Passover has not fulfilled his obligation: "Passover, unleavened bread and bitter herbs." "Passover," because God passed over the houses of our fathers in Egypt. "Unleavened bread," because our fathers were redeemed from Egypt. "Bitter herbs," because the Egyptians embittered the lives of our fathers in Egypt. In every generation, each man must regard himself as though he himself came out of Egypt. . . .

—*Rabban Gamaliel*

We were slaves to Pharoah in Egypt, but the Lord our God brought us out of there with a mighty hand and an outstretched arm. If the Holy one, praised be He, had not brought our forefathers out of Egypt, then we, our children, and our children's children would be slaves to Pharoah in Egypt.

Though all of us might be wise, all of us learned and all of us elders, though all of us might know the Torah well, it is our duty to tell the story of the exodus from Egypt. And the more one tells of the exodus from Egypt, the more praiseworthy he is. . . .

In every generation a person is obliged to see himself as though he personally came out of Egypt, as it is written, "You shall tell your son on that day saying: This is because of what the Lord did for *me* when I left Egypt." It was not our ancestors alone that the Holy One, praised be He, redeemed, but He redeemed us as well, along with them, as it is written, "He brought *us* out of there, in order to lead us to, and give us, the Land which He promised to our fathers."

Therefore are we obliged to thank, praise, laud, glorify, and exalt, to honor, bless, extol, and adore Him who performed all these wonders for our fathers and for us: He brought us out of slavery into freedom, out of sorrow into happiness, out of mourning into a holiday, out of darkness into daylight, and out of bondage into redemption. Let us then sing Him a new song: Halleluyah!

—*from the Passover*
Haggadah

Presidents' Day

(including LINCOLN'S BIRTHDAY, WASHINGTON'S BIRTHDAY)

For most of the past century, Americans celebrated the birthday of Abraham Lincoln (president, 1861–1865) on February 12, and the birthday of George Washington (president, 1789–1797) on February 22. Since 1976, the two holidays have been officially merged into Presidents' Day, the third Monday in February, when *any* former president may be honored. Thus we are spared an ever-growing number of presidential birthdays to remember!

On this occasion, share with your fellow citizens—especially children—an interesting quote from, or about, one of the great leaders from our past. The quotes below are organized into three groups:

1. ABRAHAM LINCOLN
2. GEORGE WASHINGTON
3. A SAMPLING OF OTHER PRESIDENTS

ABRAHAM LINCOLN

I know there is a God and he hates injustice and slavery. I see the storm coming and I know that His hand is in it. If He has a place and work for me—and I think He has—I believe I am ready.

—*Abraham Lincoln*

As for being President, I feel like the man who was tarred and feathered and ridden out of town on a rail. To the man who asked him how he liked it, he said, "If it wasn't for the honor of the thing, I'd rather walk."

—*Abraham Lincoln*

O, slow to smite and swift to spare!
    Gentle and merciful and just!
Who in the fear of God didst bear
    The sword of power—a nation's trust.

In sorrow by thy bier we stand
    Amid the awe that hushes all,
And speak the anguish of a land
    That shook with horror at the fall.

Thy task is done—the bonds are free;
    We bear thee to thy honored grave,
Whose proudest moments shall be
    The broken fetters of the slave.

Pure was thy life; its bloody close
Has placed thee with the sons of light,
Among the noble hosts of those
Who perished in the cause of right.
—*William Cullen Bryant*
("Lincoln")

GEORGE WASHINGTON

That I have foibles, and perhaps many of them, I shall not deny. I should esteem myself as the world also would, vain and empty, were I to arrogate perfection. . . . But this I know, and it is the highest consolation I am capable of feeling, that no man that was ever employed in a public capacity had endeavored to discharge the trust reposed in him with greater honesty and more zeal for the country's interest, than I have done.
—*George Washington*

Washington, the brave, the wise, the good,
Supreme in war, in council, and in peace,
Valiant without ambition, discreet without fear,
Confident without presumption,
In disaster, calm; in success, moderate; in all, himself;
The hero, the patriot, the Christian,
The father of nations, the friend of mankind,
Who, when he had won all, renounced all,
And sought in the bosom of his family and of nature,
    retirement,
And in the hope of religion, immortality.
—*inscription on*
Washington's tomb

First in war—first in peace—and first in the hearts of his countrymen.

—Henry Lee (about
Washington)

A SAMPLING OF OTHER PRESIDENTS

I tremble for my country when I reflect that God is just.
—Thomas Jefferson

We are imperfect. We cannot expect perfect government.
—William Howard Taft

The great voice of America does not come from the seats of learning, but in a murmur from the hills and the woods and the farms and the factories and the mills, rolling on and gaining volume until it comes to us the voice from the homes of the common men.

—Woodrow Wilson

I always figured the American public wanted a solemn ass for president, so I went along with them.

—Calvin Coolidge

Let me assert my firm belief that the only thing we have to fear is fear itself—nameless, unreasoning, unjustified terror which paralyzes needed efforts to convert retreat into advance.

—Franklin D. Roosevelt

I am proud that I am a politician. A politician is a man who understands government, and it takes a politician to run a government. A statesman is a politician who has been dead 10 or 15 years.

—Harry Truman

Sure there are dishonest men in local government. But there are dishonest men in national government too.

—Richard M. Nixon

America is never wholly herself unless she is engaged in high moral principle. We as a people have such a purpose today. It is to make kinder the face of the nation and gentler the face of the world.

—George Bush

Reunion

The quotations below are appropriate for a wide range of get-togethers, from class reunions and family reunions to any gathering of friends and/or family members who haven't seen each other for some time. Such occasions offer golden opportunities for toasting, storytelling, and invoking well-turned statements about the enduring value of human relationships. Browse among these words of wisdom and choose your favorites!

———

A friend is . . . a second self.
                    —*Cicero* (De Finnibus)

The only way to have a friend is to be one.
                    —*Ralph Waldo Emerson*

Forsake not an old friend, for the new is not comparable unto him. A new friend is as new wine: when it is old thou shalt drink it with pleasure.

—*Bible, Ecclesiasticus 9:10*

The Sight of you is good for sore Eyes.
—*Jonathan Swift*

Everybody is who he was in high school.
—*Calvin Trillin*

The language of friendship is not words but meanings.
—*Henry David Thoreau*

If the first law of friendship is that it has to be cultivated, the second law is to be indulgent when the first law has been neglected.

—*François Voltaire*

Tell me who admires and loves you,
And I will tell you who you are.
—*Charles Augustin
Sainte-Beuve*

Friendship is almost always the union of a part of one mind with a part of another; people are friends in spots.
—*George Santayana*

It is one of the blessings of old friends that you can afford to be stupid with them.

—*Ralph Waldo Emerson*

Life is partly what we make it, and partly what it is made by the friends whom we choose.

—*Tehyi Hsieh*

The bird a nest, the spider a web, man friendship.

—*William Blake*

A faithful friend is the medicine of life.

—*Bible, Ecclesiasticus*

Families are united more by mutual stories—of love and pain and adventure—than by biology. "Do you remember when . . ." bonds people together far more than shared chromosomes. Stories are thicker than blood.

—*Daniel Taylor*

Hearing and telling stories about their own family and heritage helps kids figure out how they fit in—at home and in the world.

—*Holly George-Warren*

Family discord is frequently the indirect expression of a desire for a perfect understanding.

—*Allen White*

The sense of home-coming—that strange passion for a particular set of inanimate things; or at the most for an association of ideas—has no parallel in human emotions.

—*Anonymous*

The ties of blood cannot exist without . . . constant affection.

—*Guy de Maupassant*

Children of the same family, the same blood, with the same first associations and habits, have some means of enjoyment in their power which no subsequent connections can supply.

—*Jane Austen*

You leave home to seek your fortune and when you get it you go home and share it with your family.

—*Anita Baker*

A man captured a little yellow bird in the forest, brought her home, and put her in a cage. The bird begged him, "Please let me go," but the man refused, saying, "I'll take good care of you right here."

"Very well," the bird said, "but would you at least go back to the spot where you caught me and announce that you've put me in a cage and you're going to take care of me? I just don't want my relatives to worry about me."

The man went back to that spot and made the announcement. But no sooner had he done so than one bird after another fell from the surrounding trees onto their backs on the ground, looking as dead as they could be. When he got back home and the little yellow bird asked how things had gone, the man sadly confessed, "I'm afraid the news was too much for your relatives. They fell dead at my feet!"

The little yellow bird immediately fell from her perch, onto her back on the floor of the cage, looking as dead as she could be. The man said to himself, "Birds are much too sensitive!" and sorrowfully threw the bird onto the garbage heap. But no sooner had he walked away than the bird got up, dusted herself off, and said, "You can always count on your relatives to give you good advice!" And away she flew.

—*traditional Sufi tale*

Rosh Hashanah

(also see Yom Kippur)

Rosh Hashanah, celebrated on the first day of the Jewish month of Tishri (sometime in September or October, depending on the year), begins the ten High Holy Days that culminate in Yom Kippur. This is the beginning of the new year: a time when Jews reexamine and restrengthen their relationship with God and with each other. The shofar, or ram's horn, is sounded to call the faithful to this period of judgment.

Rosh Hashanah may be solemn in many respects, but it looks forward with joy to self-renewal. It's a time when Jewish people and their friends like to exchange greetings and cards with best wishes.

We will celebrate the mighty holiness of this day, a day of awe and anxiety. On this day Your kingdom is exalted, Your throne is established in grace, and You are enthroned in truth. Truly You alone are Judge, prosecutor, investigator and witness, recorder, sealer, scribe and teller. You remember all things forgotten; You open the book of records and it tells its own story, for it is signed by the hand of every man.

The great Shofar is sounded, and a still small voice is heard. Angels are seized with fear and trembling as they proclaim: "This is the Day of Judgment!" The hosts of heaven are to be arraigned in judgment, for in Your eyes even they are not free of guilt. All who enter this world pass before you as a flock of sheep. As the shepherd musters his flock, causing each one to pass beneath his staff, so You pass and number, record and visit every living soul, setting the measure of every creature's life and decreeing his destiny.

—*from* High Holy Day
Prayer Book

Rosh Hashanah is the most universal of Jewish holidays; on it we celebrate God as father and creator of all the world, not of Israel alone. He is loving father of Ishmael, the "non-Jew" and the sinner, as much as He is of Isaac, the righteous offspring of righteous parents. As He hears the cry of the child Ishamel . . . , so He hears our cries, wherever we may be, as far as we think we are from Him.

—*Arthur Green*

Words represent the division of sound into discrete, significative units; pure sound, undifferentiated, connects directly with the undifferentiated Source of all being. On Rosh Hashanah, when the vitality of the world is reconnected with its Source, undivided and undifferentiated, the comparable sounds of the shofar serve uniquely to effect this reconnection.

—*Everett Gendler*

Fret not thyself because of evildoers, neither be thou envious against the workers of iniquity. . . .

—*Bible, Psalm 37*

May you be inscribed [in the Book of Life] for a good year.

—*traditional Rosh Hashanah*
greeting

May the good judgment be confirmed.

—*traditional greeting after*
Rosh Hashanah

Saint Patrick's Day

On March 17, the date of Saint Patrick's death in Ireland in A.D. 493, we celebrate all things Irish, regardless of our own nationality or ethnicity. Here are some quotes to help give you the gift of gab on that day, whether or not you've ever kissed the fabled Blarney stone!

The entries feature a number of greetings and toasts, the last of which you may not want to attempt unless your mind is especially sharp at the time. They also include the most famous Irish ballad set to music, "The Wearin' of the Green." It dates from the beginning of the nineteenth century, when the United Kingdom was created and any display of the Irish national symbol, the green shamrock leaf, was outlawed. Regardless of the ban, many proud Irishmen continued to sport a bit of shamrock in their cap (or "caubeen").

The Irish race is magic beyond all proportion—a small cradle, but the world for its grave.

—*Seamus O'Sullivan*

O Paddy dear, and did ye hear the news that's goin' round?
The shamrock is by law forbid to grow on Irish ground!
No more Saint Patrick's Day we'll keep, his color can't be
    seen,
For there's a cruel law ag'in the Wearin' of the Green.
I met with Napper Tandy, and he took me by the hand,
And he said, "How's poor ould Ireland, and how does she
    stand?"
She's the most distressful country that ever yet was seen,
For they're hanging men and women there for the Wearin' of
    the Green.
So of the color we must wear by England's cruel red
Let it remind us of the blood that Irishmen have shed;
And pull the shamrock from your hat, and throw it on the
    sod,
But never fear, 'twill take root there, though underfoot 'tis
    trod.
When laws can stop the blades of grass from grownin' as
    they grow,
And when the leaves in summer-time their color dare not
    show,
Then I will change the color too I wear in my caubeen;
But till that day, please God, I'll stick to the Wearin' of the
    Green.

But if at last our color should be torn from Ireland's heart,
Her sons with shame and sorrow from the dear old isle will
    part;
I've heard a whisper of a land that lies beyond the sea
Where rich and poor stand equal in the light of freedom's
    day.
O Erin, must we leave you driven by a tyrant's hand?
Must we ask a mother's blessing from a strange and distant
    land?

Where the cruel cross of England shall nevermore be seen
And where, please God, we'll live and die still Wearin' of the
    Green.

                                          —*Anonymous*

May the blessing of light be on you
Light without and light within.
May the blessed sunshine shine on you
And warm your heart till it glows like a great peat fire,
So the stranger may come and warm himself at it,
And also a friend.

And may the light shine out of the two eyes of you
Like a candle set in two windows of a house
Bidding the wanderer to come in out of the storm.

And may the blessing of the rain be on you—
The soft sweet rain.
May it fall upon your spirit
So that all the little flowers may spring up,
And shed their sweetness on the air.

And may the blessing of the earth be on you—
The great, round earth:
May you ever have a kindly greeting for them you pass
As you are going along the roads.
May the earth be soft under you when you rest upon it,
Tired at the end of the day,
And may it rest easy over you
When, at the last, you lay out under it.
May it rest so lightly over you

That your soul may be out from under it quickly—
And up and off and on its way to God.
                    —*Old Irish blessing*

May the holes in your net be no larger than the fish in it!
                    —*Irish toast*

Health to you and yours; to mine and ours.
If mine and ours ever come across you and yours,
I hope that you and yours will do as much for mine and
    ours
As mine and ours have done for you and yours.
                    —*Irish toast*

Sports Occasions

(also see BEGINNING)

In addition to offering us numerous ways to exercise our mind and body, sports also give us many chances to use our voice. Among these times for speaking up are season kickoffs, pep rallies, halftime talks, awards dinners, or simply those informal occasions when we seek to congratulate the victorious, console the defeated, or express our support and admiration for an athlete's work.

Added to these sports-oriented situations are the countless times in the course of business, work, or student life when a reference to sports seems especially appropriate. For example, we might do well to recall the fun, enterprising, or dedicated spirit of athletics when we're psyching ourselves up to face greater competition in the marketplace, or honoring an outstanding leader in our occupational field, or celebrating an individual's great academic achievement involving years of sacrifice and perseverance.

The sports-related quotations below are organized into three groups:

1. WIN OR LOSE: quotes relating to victory or defeat in athletic competition.
2. THE NATURE OF THE GAME: quotes that describe the essence of sports in general or of specific athletic endeavors.
3. PERSONAL INSIGHTS: quotes that reveal the acquired wisdom of individual athletes, coaches, or fans.

WIN OR LOSE

The following quotes are especially useful at times when you want to celebrate—or inspire—triumphs, gain a healthy perspective on setbacks, or reflect positively on an entire season of winning and losing.

––––––

You miss 100 percent of the shots you never take.
—*Wayne Gretzky*

Defeat is like a mis-cue on a pool table. In any game there's got to be a mis-cue.
—*Muhammad Ali*
(The Greatest)

It's not whether you get knocked down. It's whether you get up again.
—*Vince Lombardi*

Losers have tons of variety. Champions take pride in just learning to hit the same old boring winners.
—*Vic Braden*

Defeat should not be the source of discouragement, but a stimulus to keep plotting.

—*Shirley Chisholm*

Every time you win, you're reborn; when you lose, you die a little.

—*George Allen*

Defeat is not bitter unless you swallow it.

—*Joe Clark*

For of all sad words of tongue or pen,
The saddest are these: It might have been.

—*John Greenleaf Whittier*

I always turn to the sports pages first, which record people's accomplishments. The front page has nothing but man's failures.

—*Earl Warren*

The breakfast of champions is not cereal, it's the opposition.

—*Nick Seitz*

For when the One Great Scorer comes to write against your
name
He marks—not that you won or lost—but how you played
the game.
—*Grantland Rice*
("Alumnus Football")

Valor consists in the power of self-recovery.
—*Ralph Waldo Emerson*
(Circles)

There was ease in Casey's manner
As he stepped into his place,
There was pride in Casey's bearing
And a smile on Casey's face;

. . . .

Oh, somewhere in this favored land
The sun is shining bright,
The band is playing somewhere
And somewhere hearts are light;
And somewhere men are laughing
And somewhere children shout,
But there is no joy in Mudville;
Mighty Casey has struck out.
—*Ernest Lawrence Thayer*
("Casey at the Bat")

When valor preys on reason,
It eats the sword it fights with.
—*William Shakespeare*
(Antony and Cleopatra)

We triumph without glory when we conquer without danger.
—*Pierre Corneille* (Le Cid)

Victory goes to the player who makes the next-to-last mistake.
—*Savielly Grigorievitch*
Tartakower

Success isn't permanent, and failure isn't fatal.
—*Mike Ditka*

A good sport has to lose to prove it.
—*Anonymous*

THE NATURE OF THE GAME

Here are quotations that attempt to capture in words the special magic of sports. Even those quotes that focus on one particular kind of athletic endeavor can often be related to other kinds as well.

———

Adventure is not in the guidebook.
—*Jerry and Renny Russell*

Sport is where an entire life can be compressed into a few hours, where the emotions of a lifetime can be felt on an acre or two of ground, where a person can suffer and die and rise again on six miles of trails through a New York City park. Sport is a theater where sinner can turn saint and a common man become an uncommon hero, where the past and the future can fuse with the present. Sport is singularly able to give us peak experiences where we feel completely one with the world and transcend all conflicts as we finally become our own potential.

—*George A. Sheehan*

Here is no sentiment, no contest, no grandeur, no economics. From the sanctity of this occupation, a man may emerge refreshed and in control of his own soul. He is not idle. He is fishing, alone with himself in dignity and peace. It seems a very precious thing to me.

—*John Steinbeck*

Sports do not build character, they reveal it.

—*Heywood Hale Broun*

Racing is a game of inches and tenths of seconds. It's not any one thing you do better than the other guy, it's just that you may have mastered each little thing a little better, so you go through the corner a tenth of a second quicker.

—*Peter Revson*

Baseball is beautiful . . . the supreme performing art. It combines in perfect harmony the magnificent features of ballet, drama, art, and ingenuity.

—*Bowie Kuhn*

Laughs, kidding and ridicule are often great for a player's motivation, and motivation is the greatest mystery in any champion athlete.

—*Bill Russell* (Second Wind)

There's no game
So desperate, that the wisest of the wise
Will not take freely up for love of power,
Or love of fame, or merely love of play.

—*Sir Henry Taylor*

So you wish to conquer in the Olympic games, my friend? And I too, by the Gods, and a fine thing it would be! But first mark the conditions and the consequences, and then set to work. You will have to put yourself under discipline; to eat by rule, to avoid cakes and sweetmeats; to take exercise at the appointed hour whether you like it or not, in cold and heat; to abstain from cold drinks and from wine at your will; in a word, to give yourself over to the trainer as to a physician. Then in the conflict itself you are likely enough to dislocate your wrist or twist your ankle, to swallow a great deal of dust, or to be severely thrashed, and, after all these things, to be defeated.

—*Epictetus*
(*first century* B.C.E.)

In all times of our distress,
And in our triumph too,
The game is more than the player of the game,
And the ship is more than the crew!

—*Rudyard Kipling*

PERSONAL INSIGHTS

The following words of sports-related wisdom can raise a smile or a laugh, and sometimes even a consciousness! In tribute to baseball star Yogi Berra's famous flair with the English language, the section ends with five of his best, all-purpose quotes.

When you're as great as I am, it's hard to be humble.
        —*Muhammad Ali*

When I was in the eleventh grade, I was cut from the junior varsity basketball team (really smart coach!). Our varsity coach then approached me and asked me to play on the varsity team. "I just got cut from the JV team," I said. His answer: "I'm not coaching the JV." The moral of this story is to go with your instincts, you may just be right!
        —*Bill Russell*

Everybody is saying that I might be the most unpopular champion in the history of Wimbledon. . . . But what do I care? Because I *am* the champion!
        —*Jimmy Connors*

If you watch a game, it's fun. If you play it, it's recreation. If you work at it, it's golf.
        —*Bob Hope*

I give the same halftime speech over and over. It works best when my players are better than the other coach's players.

—*Chuck Mills*

Whenever a fellow fisherman gives the hysterical cry, "The white bass are running!" [my husband] grabs his boots and does the same. Actually I have never known the white bass to do anything else but run. They certainly never stop long enough to nibble at the bait. The reasons they give for the fish not biting are enough to stagger the imagination.

· The fish aren't biting because the water is too cold.
· The water is too hot.
· The fish are too deep.
· It is too early.
· It is too late.
· They haven't stocked it yet.
· They're up the river spawning.
· The water-skiers and motorboats have them stirred up.
· They've been poisoned by pollution.
· They just lowered the lake level.
· They haven't been biting since the Democrats have been in power.

—*Erma Bombeck*
(At Wit's End)

If you are going to try cross-country skiing, start with a small country.

—*Anonymous*

I am hunting four or five times a week here. . . . [I]t is very fine, very exciting. Even at sixty-two, I can still go harder and further and longer than some of the others. That is, I seem to have reached the point where all I have to risk is just my bones.

—*William Faulkner*

Most of us who aspire to be tops in our fields don't really consider the amount of work required to stay tops.

—*Althea Gibson*
(So Much to Live For)

For the parent of a Little Leaguer, a baseball game is simply a nervous breakdown divided into innings.

—*Earl Wilson*

It matters not whether you win or lose; what matters is whether *I* win or lose.

—*Darrin Weinberg*

Basketball develops individuality, initiative, and leadership. Now get out there and do exactly what I tell you!

—*Dick Vitale (in a pep talk as coach)*

It's like déjà vu all over again!

—*Yogi Berra (on the rehiring of Billy Martin to coach the New York Yankees)*

If people don't want to come out to the ball park, nobody's going to stop them.
— *Yogi Berra*

Predictions are difficult, especially about the future.
— *Yogi Berra*

Ninety-nine percent of the game is half mental.
— *Yogi Berra*

If you come to a fork in the road, take it.
— *Yogi Berra*

Spring

(also see BEGINNING, EASTER)

Here are some well-chosen words to welcome spring! Share them with young and old alike on any occasion, from around March 21 (the spring equinox) to around June 21 (the summer solstice). And don't forget Saint Patrick's Day or Easter, even if they don't fall officially within this period!

There is no time like Spring
When life's alive in every thing.

—Christina Rossetti ("Spring")

The green earth sends her incense up
From many a mountain shrine;
From folded leaf and dewy cup
She pours her sacred wine.

*—John Greenleaf Whittier
("The Worship of Nature")*

The year's at the spring,
And day's at the morn:
Morning's at seven;
The hill-side's dew-pearled:
The lark's on the wing,
The snail's on the thorn;
God's in his heaven—
All's right with the world.

           —*Robert Browning*
           ("Pippa Passes")

The poetry of earth is never dead; . . .
The poetry of earth is ceasing never.

           —*John Keats ("On the*
           Grasshopper and Cricket")

We listen too much to the telephone and we listen too little to nature. The [spring] wind is one of my sounds. A lonely sound, perhaps, but soothing. Everybody should have his personal sounds to listen for—sounds that will make him exhilarated and alive, or quiet and calm. . . . As a matter of fact, one of the greatest sounds of them all—and to me it is a sound—is utter, complete silence.

           —*André Kostelanetz*

The season pricketh every gentle heart,
And maketh him out of his sleep to start.

           —*Geoffrey Chaucer*

Daughter of Heaven and Earth, coy Spring,
With sudden passion languishing,
Teaching barren moors to smile,
Painting pictures mile on mile,
Holds a cup of cowslip-wreaths,
Whence a smokeless incense breathes.

—*Ralph Waldo Emerson*

A little madness in the Spring
Is wholesome even for the King,
But God be with the Clown,
Who ponders this tremendous scene—
This whole experiment in green,
As if it were his own!

—*Emily Dickinson*

Again the blackbirds sing; the streams
Wake, laughing, from their winter dreams,
And tremble in the April showers
The tassels of the maple flowers.

—*John Greenleaf Whittier*
("The Singer")

Sukkot

Sukkot, also known as the Feast of Tabernacles, is a Jewish harvest festival celebrated from Tishri 15 to 21 (usually in October). During this period, devout Jews eat in a sukkah, a booth with a roof of thatch. This pleasant but transitory structure is meant to remind them not only of the forty years when their ancestors wandered in the desert (part of the Exodus from Egypt) but also of the impermanence of life in general. The following quotes are appropriate to express or ponder during this holiday season.

From the fifteenth day of this seventh month shall be kept the feast of tabernacles, seven days to the Lord. The first day shall be a holy convocation; you shall do no servile work. Seven days you shall bring an offering made by fire to the Lord. On the eighth day shall be a holy convocation, and you shall bring an offering made by fire to the Lord. It is a day of solemn assembly; you shall do no servile work.

—*Bible, Leviticus 23:34–36*

The booth is designed to teach us not to put our trust in the size or strength or improvements of a house, nor in the help of any man, even the lord of the land, but in the Creator, for He alone is mighty, his promises alone are sure.

—*Issac Aboab*

Night falls. The family dines by candlelight and moonlight in the open air. . . . The charm of broken routine, of a new colorful way of doing familiar things, makes Sukkot a seven-day picnic—one that is dedicated and charged with symbol, as well as delightful.

—*Herman Wouk*
(This Is My God)

Now when they kept the feast of the tabernacles . . . the people . . . desired of Esdras that the laws of Moses be read to them . . . and this he did from morning to noon. . . . [T]hey were displeased at themselves and proceeded to shed tears . . . but when Esdras saw them in that disposition, he bade them go home and not weep for there was a festival. . . . He exhorted them to proceed immediately to feasting . . . but let their repentance and sorrow for their former sins be a security and guard to them.

—*Josephus*

On Sukkoth, the end of the Days of Repentance, the Torah advises us to accept the exile and to consider all the world as void, as a shadow. Therefore we are told to leave permanent dwellings for a temporary one, to teach that we are strangers on the earth, without permanence, and that our days are like a shadow lasting a night, blown away by a wind. What does a man profit from all his labors under the sun? All his days let his eyes be on high to the One who dwells in the heavens. Therefore one must use twigs and branches for the roof of the Sukkah, that the stars be clearly visible from inside it, that one might direct his heart to heaven.

—*J. Eibschultz*

Summer

Summer supposedly starts around June 21, the summer solstice, and ends around September 21, the fall equinox. Most of us, however, think of summer as the season between Memorial Day (May 30) and Labor Day (the first Monday in September). Whenever you celebrate it—or one of its days, like the Fourth of July or a summertime birthday—do so with some of the following words.

———

And what is so rare as a day in June?
Then, if ever, come perfect days;
Then Heaven tries the earth if it be in tune,
And over it softly her warm ear lays.
                              —*James Russell Lowell*
                              ("The Vision of Sir Launfal")

"Summer is coming, summer is coming,
I know it, I know it, I know it.
Light again, leaf again, life again, love again,"
Yes, my wild little Poet.

Sing the new year in under the blue.
Last year you sang it as gladly.
"New, new, new, new!" Is it then *so* new
That you should carol so madly?

"Love again, song again, nest again, young again!"
Never a prophet so crazy!
And hardly a daisy as yet, little friend,
See, there is hardly a daisy.

"Hear again, here, here, here, happy year!"
O warble unchidden, unbidden!
Summer is coming, is coming, my dear,
And all the winters are hidden.

     —Alfred, Lord Tennyson

When the green woods laugh with the voice of joy,
And the dimpling stream runs laughing by;
When the air does laugh with our merry wit,
And the green hill laughs with the noise of it;

When the meadows laugh with lively green,
And the grasshopper laughs in the merry scene,
When Mary and Susan and Emily
With their sweet round mouths sing "Ha, Ha, He!"

When the painted birds laugh in the shade,
Where our table with cherries and nuts is spread,

Come live and be merry, and join with me,
To sing the sweet chorus of "Ha, Ha, He!"
—*William Blake*

Pride of summer passing by
With lordly laughter in her eye.
—*Algernon Swinburne*
("The Tale of Balin")

Before green apples blush,
Before green nuts embrown,
Why, one day in the country
Is worth a month in town.

—*Christina Rossetti*
("Summer")

'Tis the last rose of summer,
Left blooming alone;
All her lovely companions
Are faded and gone.

—*Thomas Moore*

Thanksgiving Day

(also see Autumn)

The fourth Thursday in November is a day set aside to count our blessings as individuals, families, and Americans. It's been a tradition since the Pilgrims of Plymouth sat down to dinner with their Native American neighbors in 1623, and an official annual holiday since George Washington proclaimed it one in 1789. Spread these words to lend a special grace to the occasion!

Inasmuch as the great Father has given us this year an abundant harvest of Indian corn, wheat, beans, squashes, and garden vegetables, and has made the forests to abound with game and the sea with fish and clams, and inasmuch as He has . . . granted us freedom to worship God according to the dictates of our own conscience; now I . . . do proclaim that all ye Pilgrims . . . render thanksgiving to ye Almighty God for His blessings.

—*William Bradford (governor*
of the Massachusetts Bay
Colony, 1623)

Let us come before his presence with Thanksgiving.
—*Bible, Psalm 95:2*

Thanksgiving Day comes, by statute, once a year; to the honest man it comes as frequently as the heart of gratitude will allow, which may mean every day, or at least once in seven days.

—*Edward Sandford Martin*

Thou hast given so much to me,
Give one thing more,—a grateful heart;
Not thankful when it pleaseth me,
As if Thy blessings had spare days,
But such a heart whose pulse may be Thy praise.

—*George Herbert*

Almighty God, Father of all mercies, we Thine unworthy servants do give Thee most humble and hearty thanks for all Thy goodness and loving-kindness to us, and to all men. We bless Thee for our creation, preservation, and all the blessings of this life; but above all, for Thine inestimable love in the redemption of the world by our Lord Jesus Christ; for the means of grace, and for the hope of glory. And, we beseech Thee, give us that due sense of all Thy mercies, that our hearts may be unfeignedly thankful; and that we show forth Thy praise, not only with our lips, but in our lives, by giving up our selves to Thy service, and by walking before Thee in holiness and righteousness all our days; through Jesus Christ our Lord, to whom, with Thee and the Holy Ghost, be all honor and glory, world without end. Amen.

—*Book of Common Prayer*

A thankful heart is not only the greatest virtue, but the parent of all the other virtues.

—*Cicero*

We are grateful for the plentiful yield of our soil. . . . We rejoice in the beauty of our land. . . . We deeply appreciate the preservation of those ideals of liberty and justice which form the basis of our national life, and the hope of international peace. . . .

Let us be especially grateful for the religious heritage bequeathed us by our forefathers, as exemplified by the Pilgrims, who, after the gathering of their first harvest, set apart a special day for rendering thanks to God for the bounties vouchsafed to them. . . .

—*Dwight David Eisenhower*

All over the land and far over the sea
Our glad "gobble-gobble" is heard,
'Tis the national air of the brave and the free
The song of the Thanksgiving bird!

—*John Howard Jewett*

Anyone can count the seeds in an apple. Only God can count the apples in a seed.

—*Robert H. Schuller*

Ah! on Thanksgiving day, when from East and from West,
From North and South, come the pilgrim and guest,
When the gray-haired New Englander sees round his board
The old broken links of affection restored,
When the care-wearied man seeks his mother once more,
And the worn matron smiles where the girl smiled before.
What moistens the lips and what brightens the eye?
What calls back the past, like the rich pumpkin pie?

—*John Greenleaf Whittier*

Valentine's Day

(Saint Valentine's Day; also see Anniversary, Wedding)

The history behind this date is given below, in the first entry. Suffice it to say that its sole reason for being is to compel you to speak of your love—loud and proud—even if you fail to do so on any other day of the year. May the words offered here loosen your tongue or pen to share what's in your heart!

In pre-Christian times the lottery technique was employed at the feast of Juno Februaria, February 15. On that day it was thought that the birds chose their mates for the season. By a form of sympathetic magic boys and girls would draw lots for one another. . . . When Christianity took over . . . the date was shifted to February 14, and the honor given to Valentinus, a priest who was condemned by Emperor Claudius II to be beaten, stoned, and then beheaded. While awaiting execution he is said to have formed a friendship with the blind daughter of his jailor, to whom he wrote a note on the eve of his death, signed, "From your Valentine." The date was February 14, A.D. 270.

—*Arthur Calder-Marshall*

I have spread no snares today. I am caught in my love of you.

> —*Egyptian proverb*

Good morrow! 'Tis St. Valentine's Day
  All in the morning betime
And I a maid at your window
  To be your valentine.

> —*William Shakespeare*
> (Hamlet)

The moon shall be a darkness
  The stars give no light,
If ever I prove false
  To my heart's delight;
In the middle of the ocean
  Green grow the myrtle tree,
If ever I prove false
  To my Love that loves me.

> —*Anonymous*

Till a' the seas gang dry, my dear,
  And the rocks melt wi' the sun;
I will luve thee still, my dear,
  While the sands o' life shall run.

> —*Robert Burns ("My Luve's*
> *Like a Red, Red Rose")*

Do you love me
Or do you not?
You told me once
But I forgot.

—*Anonymous*

I love you more than my own skin.

—*Frida Kahlo*

When one is in love, a cliff becomes a meadow.

—*Ethiopian proverb*

Love is never ending. Love is always.

—*Smokey Robinson*

And on her lover's arm she leant,
And round her waist she felt it fold,
And far across the hills they went
In that new world which is the old.

—*Alfred, Lord Tennyson*

Love has never cared about my schedule. It just barges in
whenever it wants.

—*Miriam Makeba* (My Story)

A hundred hearts would be too few
To carry all my love for you
The one I send is true as gold
And gives itself a hundred fold.

              —Anonymous

With love's light wings did I o'er perch these walls.
For stony limits cannot hold love out,
And what love can do that dares love attempt.

              —William Shakespeare
              (Romeo and Juliet)

Hearing your voice is pomegranate wine,
I live by hearing it.
Each look with which you look at me
Sustains me more than food and drink.

              —Egyptian proverb

Veterans Day

(Armistice Day; also see Memorial Day)

Veterans Day began its history as Armistice Day—November 11, 1918—when a cease-fire ending World War I was signed by the Allied Forces and Germany in the French forest of Compiègne. In 1921, the date was additionally solemnized with the burial of the American Unknown Soldier (an unidentified body) in Washington, D.C.'s Arlington National Cemetery.

By a 1954 act of Congress, the Armistice Day anniversary was renamed Veterans Day in order to honor servicepeople in all of America's wars. Since that time, an unidentified body from each armed conflict has been buried in what is now called the Tomb of the Unknowns.

Veterans Day is a time of parades, banquets, memorial services, graveside visits, and special ceremonies at home. The following quotations will help you to honor a particular veteran, or all American veterans, on this very important occasion.

Blessed is that country whose soldiers fight for it and are willing to give the best they have, the best that any man has, their own lives to preserve it because they love it. Such an army the United States has always commanded in every crisis of her history.

—*William McKinley*

Americanism means the virtues of courage, honor, justice, truth, sincerity, and hardihood—the things that made America. The things that will destroy America are prosperity at any price, peace at any price, safety first instead of duty first, the love of soft living, and the get-rich theory of life.

—*Theodore Roosevelt*

Ask not what your country can do for you. Rather, ask what you can do for your country.

—*John F. Kennedy*

In Flanders fields the poppies grow
Between the crosses, row on row,
That mark our place, and in the sky,
The larks, still bravely singing, fly,
Scarce heard amid the guns below.

—*John McCrae*

It is a sweet and proper thing to die for one's country.

—*Horace* (Latin: *"Dulce et decorum est pro patria mori."*)

A solemn inscription [on the Tomb of the Unknowns]: a nation's promise that he who lies there dead shall not have died in vain.

The world has made the promise before; all its unknown dead have died in that faith. And the promise has died with them.

Will it die again?

We told that boy when he marched away that he was fighting a war to end all wars. He fell, believing; and we have buried him and carved an inscription over his tomb.

But the real inscription will not be written on any stone; it will stand in the dictionaries of the future. Only by writing it thus can the world keep faith with the long sad procession of its unknown heroes whom it has lied to and cheated and fooled.

This will be the inscription:

War
An Armed Contest Between Nations—
Now Obsolete
Unknown

                       —*Bruce Barton*

Soldier, rest! thy warfare o'er,
Sleep the sleep that knows not breaking;
Dream of battled fields no more,
Days of danger, nights of waking.

                       —*Sir Walter Scott*

The nation which forgets its defenders will be itself forgotten.
                       —*Calvin Coolidge*

Wedding

❦

(also see ANNIVERSARY, BEGINNING, VALENTINE'S DAY)

Depending on the individual couple, a wedding may involve not just a marriage ceremony but also an engagement party, bridal shower, bachelor party, rehearsal dinner, and innumerable minor but still celebratory meals, visits, toasts, notes, and get-togethers in between. Here are plenty of things to be said on such occasions, whether you're a bride, groom, or innocent bystander.

The quotations below are divided into three different groups:

1. LOVE BETWEEN TWO PEOPLE: quotes that speak of the special bond shared by two people intent upon marrying each other.
2. THE MARRIAGE ADVENTURE: quotes regarding the nature of marriage itself, including words of advice and blessing.
3. LIGHTHEARTED REMARKS: humorous asides on marriage or the people who seek it, to be shared with tongue in cheek.

LOVE BETWEEN TWO PEOPLE

Therefore shall a man leave his father and his mother, and shall cleave unto his wife, and they shall be one flesh.

—*Bible, Genesis 2:24*

It is only with the heart that one can see rightly; what is essential is invisible to the eye.

—*Antoine de Saint-Exupéry*

Husband and wife are like the two equal parts of a soybean. If the two parts are put under the earth separately, they will not grow. The soybean will grow only when the parts are covered by the skin. Marriage is the skin which covers each of them and makes them one.

—*Indian expression*

You and I
Have so much love,
That it
Burns like a fire,
In which we bake a lump of clay
Molded into a figure of you
And a figure of me.
Then we take both of them,
And break them into pieces,
And mix the pieces with water,
And mold again a figure of you,
And a figure of me.

I am in your clay.
You are in my clay.
In life we share a single quilt.
In death we will share one coffin.

—*Kuan Tao-sheng*

When you really want love you will find it waiting for you.
—*Oscar Wilde*
(De Profundis)

It would be impossible to "love" anyone or anything one knew *completely*. Love is directed towards what lies hidden in its object.

—*Paul Valéry* (Tel Quel)

Let your love be like the misty rains, coming softly, but flooding the river.

—*Malagasy proverb*

Love stretches your heart and makes you big inside.
—*Margaret Walker* (Jubilee)

Love is the most durable power in the world.
—*Martin Luther King, Jr.*

Love does not dominate; it cultivates.
—*Johann Wolfgang*
von Goethe

Love is space and time made directly perceptible to the heart.
—*Marcel Proust*

Love does not consist in gazing at each other but in looking
together in the same direction.
—*Antoine de Saint-Exupéry*

How do I love thee? Let me count the ways.
I love thee to the depth and breadth and height
My soul can reach, when feeling out of sight
For the end of Being and Ideal Grace.
I love thee to the level of everyday's
Most quiet need, by sun and candlelight.
I love thee freely, as men strive for Right;
I love thee purely, as they turn from Praise.
I love thee with the passion put to use
In my old griefs, and with my childhood's faith.
I love thee with a love I seemed to lose
With my lost saints,—I love thee with the breath,
Smiles, tears, of all my life!—and, if God choose,
I shall but love thee better after death.
—*Elizabeth Barrett Browning*

In love the paradox occurs that two beings become one and
yet remain two.
—*Erich Fromm*

The meeting of two personalities is like the contact of two
chemical substances; if there is any reaction, both are trans-
formed.
—*Carl Jung*

Wither thou goest, I will go.

—*Bible, Ruth*

Drink to me only with thine eyes,
And I will pledge with mine;
Or leave a kiss but in the cup,
And I'll not look for wine.

—*Ben Jonson*

That your love knot may be sealed with heaven's wax!

—*Irish toast*

THE MARRIAGE ADVENTURE

All tragedies are finish'd by a death,
All comedies are ended by a marriage.

—*George Gordon, Lord
Byron ("Don Juan")*

Marriage is like a three-speed gearbox: affection, friendship, love. It is not advisable to crash your gears and go right through to love straightaway. You need to ease your way through. The basis of love is respect, and that needs to be learned from affection and friendship.

—*Peter Ustinov*

Women deprived of the company of men pine, men deprived of the company of women become stupid.

—*Anton Chekhov*

The kindest and the happiest pair
Will find occasion to forbear,
And something every day they live
To pity, and perhaps forgive.

—*William Cowper*

Just pray for a thick skin and a tender heart.

—*Ruth Graham (wife of*
evangelist Billy Graham)

Love is blind, but marriage restores its sight.

—*Samuel Lichtenberg*
(Aphorisms)

May you have enough happiness to keep you sweet; enough trials to keep you strong; enough sorrow to keep you human; enough hope to keep you happy; enough failure to keep you humble; enough success to keep you eager; enough friends to give you comfort; enough faith and courage in yourself, your business, and your country to banish depression; enough wealth to meet your needs; enough determination to make each day a better day than yesterday.

—*Anonymous*

Here's to matrimony, the high sea for which no compass has yet been invented!

—*Heinrich Heine*

LIGHTHEARTED REMARKS

Husbands are like fires. They go out if unattended.
—*Zsa Zsa Gabor*

The reason husbands and wives do not understand each other is because they belong to different sexes.
—*Dorothy Dix*

I have learned only two things are necessary to keep one's wife happy. First, let her think she is having her own way. Second, let her have it.
—*Anthony Armstrong-Jones*

It was so cold I almost got married.
—*Shelley Winters*

Love is a sport in which the hunter must contrive to have the quarry in pursuit.
—*Alphonse Kerr*

Never go to bed mad. Stay up and fight.
—*Phyllis Diller*

One should never know too precisely whom one has married.
—*Friedrich Nietzsche*

My boyfriend and I broke up. He wanted to get married and I didn't want him to.

—*Rita Rudner*

Love is the only game that is not called on account of darkness.

—*Max Hirschfield*

As I ever hope to drink wine or ale, I'll tell you the truth of the husbands that I have married, three were good and two were bad. The three good ones were rich and old; they could scarcely hold to the contract by which they were bound to me. You know very well what I mean by this, by God! So help me God, I laugh when I think how pitifully I made them work at night! And, by my faith, I gave them no credit for it. . . . But I managed them so well by my own rules that each of them was blissfully happy and glad to bring me gay things from the fair.

—*Geoffrey Chaucer*
(Canterbury Tales, "The
Wife of Bath's Tale")

He has a future and I have a past, so we should be all right.

—*Jennie Churchill (at age 64,*
on her marriage to
Montague Porch, 41—three
years younger than her son
Winston)

Any young man who is unmarried at the age of twenty-one is a menace to the community.

—*Brigham Young*

If it weren't for marriage, men and women would have to fight with total strangers.

—*Anonymous*

Love is being stupid together.

—*Paul Valéry*

In a great romance, each person basically plays a part that the other really likes.

—*Elizabeth Ashley*

Marriage is popular because it provides the maximum of temptation with the maximum of opportunity.

—*George Bernard Shaw*

Marriage halves our griefs, doubles our joys, and quadruples our expenses.

—*Anonymous*

Marrying a man is like buying something you've been admiring for a long time in a shop window. You may love it when you get it home, but it doesn't always go with everything else in the house.

—*Jean Kerr*

When a woman gets married it's like jumping into a hole in the ice in the middle of winter: you do it once, and you remember it the rest of your days.

—*Alexander Bakshy*

A man in love is incomplete until he is married. Then he is finished.

—*Zsa Zsa Gabor*

An ideal wife is any woman who has an ideal husband.
—*Booth Tarkington*

Winter

Winter reigns from around December 21 (winter solstice) to around March 21 (spring equinox), or so goes the calendar. Where you live, it may come earlier and stay later. While it's around, here are some illuminating, if not always warm, things to say about it!

I save writing for the four months of bad weather from December through April, when there's nothing else to do. I never take up serious writing in good weather. I'm outdoors too much.

—*William Faulkner*

Announced by all the trumpets of the sky,
Arrives the snow, and, driving o'er the fields,
Seems nowhere to alight: the whited air
Hides hills and woods, the river, and the heaven,
And veils the farmhouse at the garden's end.

The sled and traveller stopped, the courier's feet
Delayed, all friends shut out, the housemates sit
Around the radiant fireplace, enclosed
In a tumultuous privacy of storm.

> —*Ralph Waldo Emerson*
> *("The Snow-storm")*

O Winter, rule of th' inverted year, . . .
I crown thee king of intimate delights,
Fire-side enjoyments, home-born happiness,
And all the comforts that the lowly roof
Of undisturb'd retirement, and the long hours
Of long uninterrupted ev'ning, know.

> —*William Cowper*
> *("The Task")*

I like winter because I can stay indoors without feeling guilty.

> —*Teresa Skelton*

Winter tames man, woman, and beast.

> —*William Shakespeare*
> (The Taming of the Shrew)

O the snow, the beautiful snow,
Filling the sky and earth below;
Over the house-tops, over the street,
Over the heads of the people you meet,
Dancing, flirting, skimming along.

> —*James W. Watson*
> *("Beautiful Snow")*

In the winter the earth is pregnant. It bears within itself a great secret. In the summer, the secret is disclosed.

—*Rabbi Nachman of Bratislava*

O, wind,
If Winter comes, can Spring be far behind?

—*Percy Bysshe Shelley*
("Prometheus Unbound")

Yom Kippur

(also see Rosh Hashanah)

Yom Kippur ends the ten-day period of repentance for Jews that begins with Rosh Hashanah (Tishri 1 to 10, around September-October). It's a day when devout Jews offer final prayers of atonement for their sins and ask God to forgive them. In ancient ritual, the sins were symbolically loaded onto a goat that was then driven away—hence, the common image of a "scapegoat."

On this highest of Jewish holy days, the new year is begun with a clean slate. Consider and utter these words, as you rejoice in the spirit of a fresh beginning.

On the tenth day of this seventh month shall be the Day of Atonement. There shall be a holy convocation to you, and you shall afflict your souls, and you shall bring forth an offering made by fire to the Lord. You shall do no servile work in this day, for it is a day of atonement, to make atonement for you before the Lord your God.

—Bible, Leviticus 23:27–32

Like the clay in the hand of the potter
Who thickens or thins it at his will,
So are we in Thy hand, gracious God,
Forgive our sin, Thy covenant fulfill.

Like a stone in the hand of the mason
Who preserves or breaks it at his will,
So we are in Thy hand, Lord of life,
Forgive our sin, Thy covenant fulfill.

Like iron in the hand of the craftsman
Who forges or cools it at his will,
We are in Thy hand, O Keeper,
Forgive our sin, Thy covenant fulfill.

Like the wheel in the hand of the seaman
Who directs or holds it at his will
So are we in Thy hand, loving God,
Forgive our sin, Thy covenant fulfill.

Like the glass in the hand of the blower
Who dissolves or shapes it at his will,
So are we in Thy hand, God of grace,
Forgive our sin, Thy covenant fulfill.

Like the cloth in the hand of the tailor
Who smoothens or drapes it at his will,
So are we in Thy hand, righteous God,
Forgive our sin, Thy covenant fulfill.

Like silver in the hand of the smelter
Who refines or blends it at his will,
So are we in Thy hand, our Healer,
Forgive our sin, Thy covenant fulfill.

—*Anonymous*

Yom Kippur is no longer a day of repentance in its primary focus. Rather, it is a day when those who have failed at repentance—and which of us had not?—may cast themselves upon God's mercies and ask that He act for them. Until this final day of the season of repentance, all is up to us; it is we who are given the burden of changing our ways.

—*Arthur Green*

Our God and God of our fathers, let our prayer come before You. Hide not from our supplication, for we are neither so brazen nor so arrogant as to say before You, O Lord our God and God of our fathers, "We are righteous and have not sinned"; truly we have sinned. . . .

You know the mysteries of the universe, and the hidden secrets of all living. You search out the innermost reasons and probe the heart and mind. Nothing is concealed from You, or hidden from your sight.

May it therefore be Your will, O Lord our God and God of our fathers, to forgive us for all our sins, to pardon us for all our iniquities, and to grant us atonement for all our transgressions.

—*from the High Holy Days
Prayer Book*